Praise for
The Main Thing: 40 Days of Grace

Clay and I both share enthusiasm for adventure whether it is camping, motorcycles, or overlanding. But we also are both committed to the greatest adventure of all, which is helping people find true freedom in Christ. Allow Clay to be your guide on a tour of Galatians for the next forty days.

— Brian Tome, Senior Pastor, Crossroads Church, and author of *The Five Marks of a Man*

Far too many Christians are spiritual and miserable. The root causes of that all begin with "G": Guilt, Grief, and Grudges— the main culprit usually being Guilt. Clay Peck has done the Christian Church a great service with his brand–new book, *The Main Thing*. I am praying that God will use this to set Christians free from guilt and the past. Imagine what American Christianity would look like if Christians were liberated!

— Ray Johnston, Senior Pastor, Bayside Church, Founder of Thrive Communications, Inc., and Thriving Churches International, and author of *Hope Quotient*

In *The Main Thing* Clay serves as a sherpa, taking us on a journey along the narrow path toward freedom, which is edged by the dangerous abyss of *legalism* on one side and *license* on the other. As Clay and I envisioned what a three–dimensional Grace Place could look, taste, and feel like for the "Samaritan women" of today on the high plains of Colorado, I saw him live this out through a journey fraught with trials and tribulations, highs and lows, but always marked by grace. Clay, thank you for all the baggage you've taught me to leave behind, my friend.

— **Mel McGowan, AICP, DBIA, LEED AP, Founder, PlainJoe Studios, Master Planner & Designer: Grace Place, and author of *Design Intervention* and *Sacred Storytellers***

Explain. Illustrate. Apply. Clay Peck masterfully uses this approach to fix our eyes on Jesus and the pure gospel he proclaimed and demonstrated. I've been to Grace Place and can attest that the church is welcoming and transforming, not closed and condemning. Grace, peace, and freedom in Christ await you in these thoughtful reflections on Galatians.

— **Dr. John Wenrich, President The Evangelical Covenant Church**

The Main Thing: 40 Days of Grace is a great read for anyone trying to boil down exactly what it means to be Christian. Clay supports the Main Thing from forty different angles, with biblical support and commonsense truth in each day's reading. Peck challenges believers to hold tight to the main thing while so many try to add to and amend what it means to be Christian. This is a well–written book with inspiring truths for the beginner and the long–time Christian.

— **Karl Mecklenburg, former Denver Bronco All-Pro Linebacker, motivational speaker, and author of *Heart of a Student Athlete***

Prepare to be blessed as Clay guides you in this study of God's Word. Living a life with Jesus as Lord has filled me with joy and sustained me through some difficult times. I have often trusted Clay as my guide. He absolutely has a true heart for Christ and for all people. Prepare to be blessed!

— **Joe Tanner, former NASA Astronaut**

Firstly, my friend Clay Peck models every segment of this book in his life and leadership. And because Clay's character reflects the character of Christ, we need to listen to what he has to say. Secondly, *Grace Place,* the church God has entrusted Clay to lead, is sold out to corporately living the biblical principles espoused in this book. I encourage you to make *The Main Thing* your main thing!

— **Greg Nettle, President, Stadia Church Planting**

I have known Clay Peck for a couple of decades. The church he leads is called Grace Place for a reason. His passion is to reveal the grace of our God to those who least expect it. He has been on a relentless pursuit to present a gospel that will free people from their guilt and shame. A must read!

— **Dary Northrup, Senior Pastor Timberline Church**

Clay Peck is a world–class leader. His pastoral heart for people shines through in his leadership and life and is profoundly expressed in every word of this great book. In his book, *The Main Thing: 40 Days of Grace,* Pastor Clay invites us to reject life in the "law place" and embrace true life firmly planted in God's "grace place." Let this book move you forward into the way of life to which Jesus has called you.

— **Jonathan Wiggins, Lead Pastor, Rez Church, and author of *Walking with Lions***

Clay not only has "The Main Thing..." and an image of a cross tattooed on his arms, he has them tattooed on his heart—and on his mind and his tongue. Using the book of Galatians as his stencil, he has now inked the message of God's grace and gospel so they can be permanently engraved in your life.

— **Brian Mavis, President, America's Kids Belong**

If you are looking for details and debates, look somewhere else. In this devotional Clay keeps "the main thing the main thing." *Jesus* is what Christianity is all about. Not judgement, not rules, not politics, not smug self-righteousness. If you're tired of being distracted by all the "add-ons" to Christianity that seem to subtract more than they add, this devotional will point you back to why people for a thousand generations have joyfully devoted their lives to following Jesus.

— **Pastor Dave Swaim**
President of the Highrock Network of Churches

Clay is a great leader and a gifted pastor, and he has an unwavering commitment to what is most important in the life of a disciple of Jesus Christ. Whether or not you agree with everything Clay writes as he takes us on a journey through Galatians, you will certainly be challenged and invited to reflect on who Jesus is and what he has done for us. May your reading and reflection draw you closer to the One who gave it all for you and me.

— **Tammy Swanson-Draheim, Pastor and**
Superintendent of the Midwest Conference of the
Evangelical Covenant Church

When Clay asked me to endorse his new book I immediately replied: "I would always endorse you. . . and anything else you wanted me to!" After nearly twenty-five years of friendship, and enjoying a close connection in our three–year soul care Covenant Group, I trust Clay Peck! His journey of grace isn't just a heady intellectual one, it is an intensely personal heartfelt one. Having read his entire manuscript, I highly endorse this forty–day devotional and look forward to rereading and pondering it again. Clay writes with the careful insight of a theologian and the genuine heart of a tested pastor and sincere Christ follower. My only lament is that he didn't finish this soul–enriching resource much sooner! The vocabulary Clay provides is truly life giving for all who need to be reminded that *the position of Savior has been taken!*

— Dr. Alan Ahlgrim, Founding Pastor, Rocky Mountain Christian Church, Chief SoulCare Officer, Covenant-Connections.org

Clay's passion for the gospel was a breath of fresh air to my soul. What a biblically rooted and powerful reminder to keep the gospel the main thing, and what an inspiring invitation for all of us to experience true freedom. I urge you to read this book and rediscover all that the simple gospel of Christ offers you.

— Alan Kraft, Senior Pastor, Christ Community Church (cccgreeley.org) and author of *More: When a Little Bit of the Spirit is not Enough*, and *Good News for Those Trying Harder*

We live in a world where we feel overwhelmed by so many things vying for our time and attention. In *The Main Thing* my friend Clay Peck guides us through a forty-day journey that helps us get clear on what God's good news is and is not. Clay leads us through the letter to the Galatians where we realize that 2000 years ago just like today, Christians were getting confused about what is essential and what is secondary. Do you want more freedom, peace, and life? Read this book prayerfully, and keep the main thing the main thing.

— **Alex Rahill, Director of Church Planting**
The Evangelical Covenant Church

Do you feel defeated or distant from God in any way? Chances are you're not experiencing the full benefits of God's grace. To know God's grace is to know his heart. Clay shows us through scripture and practical examples how to live *from* God's victory rather than striving *toward* victory!

— **Tom Ewing, Worship Consultant**
Kingdom Encourager

What a refreshing and well–written book! Grounded in Galatians, this is such a needed read for our time. Peck's captivating and well–written style motivates us to cherish the gospel of Christ while navigating the peripheral hazards of legalism and license. Don't just scan this compelling study! Read it, share it, and celebrate God's amazing grace anew!

— Chaplain Lieutenant Colonel Randy Croft

Clay Peck is the real deal. He doesn't just talk about grace, he lives it, his church exudes it, and his life bears the fruit of it. His experience in an ultra-legalistic church structure gives him a unique perspective and credibility in guiding us down this road as he helps us understand the difference between the yoke of religion and the freedom we find in Christ. I can't wait for you to experience the liberation in putting the "main thing" in its place and letting everything else fall to the wayside.

— Angel Flores, Lead Pastor, Mosaic Church

I have witnessed Clay Peck focusing on "the main thing" for more than twenty-five years. By lifting up Christ, above all, and encouraging us to look and live, he has made genuine and lasting impact—eternal impact—in the lives of many, including me. Grace Place is indeed the perfect name for the groundbreaking community that he helped gather together and continues to shepherd, a place where the ground is still level at the foot of the cross, where hope and healing flow freely and new life abounds.

**— Rik Swartzwelder,
writer-director of *Old Fashioned***

THE MAIN THING

THE MAIN THING

40 DAYS OF GRACE

CLAY PECK

MEDIA.COM

THE MAIN THING

Published by
Illumify Media Global
www.IllumifyMedia.com
"Let's bring your book to life!"

Library of Congress Control Number: 2021913199

Paperback ISBN: 978-1-955043-24-3
eBook ISBN: 978-1-955043-25-0

Typeset by Art Innovations (http://artinnovations.in/)
Cover design by Debbie Lewis

Printed in the United States of America

DEDICATION

To my dear wife, Selene, who encouraged me to write this book, gave me many editorial suggestions, and has faithfully supported my ministry for nearly four decades.

To the congregation called Grace Place who have allowed me to teach God's Word and responded like the Bereans, "for they received the message with great eagerness" (Acts 17:11).

To Richard Fredericks, long time mentor and friend, who helped me discover the centrality of the gospel and graciously wrote the foreword.

CONTENTS

FOREWORD
BY DR. RICHARD FREDERICKS

Near the end of this book, author Clay Peck cites a story from Doris Kearns-Goodwin's Pulitzer-Prize winning biography on Abraham Lincoln *Team of Rivals*. On January 1, 1863, as he is about to sign the Emancipation Proclamation—declaring freedom for the slaves of an entire nation—Lincoln realizes his hand is trembling from weariness. He puts down his pen, saying: "If my hand trembles when I sign this Proclamation, all who examine it will say, 'He hesitated.'"

So Lincoln waits until he can sign with a firm hand. Clearly, Clay's hand was not trembling when he wrote this book. He offers us the very truth he lives by and would die for. He bears its marks on his body (more on that in Day One's reading). In the pages ahead Clay wrestles with, and revels in, the apostle Paul's defense of the gospel in his letter to the Galatians.

Consider what is at stake *for you* in this book: IF what it contains is true, or even IF it is *perhaps* true. . . then nothing else in your life matters so much. Front to back, *The Main Thing* explores the one true "gospel" (declaration of good news) that stands alone at the heart of Christianity. The apostle Paul declares, in his letter to the Romans, a more reflective counterpart to the white–hot, bare–knuckle passion of his letter to the Galatians: "I am not ashamed of the gospel, for it is the power of God for salvation to everyone who believes" (Romans 1:16 NASB).

Please note two very important things in this declaration which Clay will explore. First, Paul is not declaring *a gospel*, his personal favorite among many good options. Paul is clear. He is declaring "*the* gospel." There is just one. There is no other.

And second, this one and only gospel offers us "*the power of God for salvation.*" Once again, there is no option B. God's power to redeem and restore our complete humanity and sanity, and open up to us eternity, flows through Jesus Christ to us in *just one way.*

Clay explores how, in Galatians, Paul declares, defines, and defends this one gospel by answering two primary questions:

- What is this one true gospel of God (and why it alone can save us)?
- What is the freedom it offers (and why it alone is true freedom)?

Big claims! If they are true, the stakes could not be higher. Paul is so sure this gospel is God's one offered way of salvation, he states not once but twice, right at the front door of Galatians, that if anyone anywhere, even an angel from heaven, tries to offer "another gospel" they stand eternally condemned (Galatians 1:7-9).

Often good teachers briefly tell you what they are going to tell you; then explain it to you clearly and carefully, and finally they tell you again what they told you. Repetition deepens impression. Let me tell you briefly where Clay will clearly and carefully take you in the pages ahead.

Clay will tell you the gospel is not at all about you and what you can do for God. The gospel is entirely about God and what he has done for you in Jesus Christ. Specifically, the gospel is what Jesus has achieved for us by his victorious sacrifice on the Cross and by his defeat of death at the empty tomb. This is God's sole saving power for humanity. It is utterly *ex*clusive: there is only one gospel. And it is utterly *in*clusive: it is for everyone, everywhere. It is for you.

Clay will carefully explain how in Christ we live and serve from victory—not toward it. Eternity has already been won by One. Clay will demonstrate the gospel of Galatians is:

- **Historical**—it is not good advice, it is the good news of a past event: the declaration of Jesus' death and resurrection for our salvation.
- **Finished**—The gospel is not an ongoing process. It is a completed gift from God.
- **Perfect**—nothing we do can add to a single thing to the fullness of what Christ has done or take anything away from its saving power. Our only part is to follow or reject the risen LORD who has provided "so great a salvation" (Hebrews 2:3).

Our acceptance before God rests completely on this finished and perfect work of Christ alone. Plus nothing. Period. Only on this foundation can we build securely—for eternity.

And Clay will carefully show us there is more: The *root* of the gospel grows *fruit* in every trusting life. When we come to Christ—just as we are—we will not stay just as we are. He will heal us and restore us to who we were created to be. The smallest package in the whole world is a man (or woman) wrapped up in himself. But by his self-sacrificial love, Jesus sets us free from the very essence of sin: our intense preoccupation with ourselves as our own frail little "gods" in our own frail little world.

The heart of Galatians is echoed in Hebrews 10:14: "For by one sacrifice he has made perfect forever those who are being made holy." To amplify: by one sacrifice [the Cross], he [Jesus] *has* [not will, but has] *made us* perfect forever; even while we are *still becoming* holy—while we are still learning what this infinite Gift means for every part of our life.

John Wesley loved to say: "By the gospel, we are perfectly God's children long before we are perfect children of God." To reach God, religion tells us to do and do and do; but the gospel declares our salvation in Christ is done.

Finally, Clay will show us how the psychological genius of God's grace shapes our daily living. Individually and as the community, as we live by our trust in Christ, we become increasingly a "cruciform"— people shaped by the Cross in every part of our life together.

Listen: God knows well it is cruel to ask an insecure person to live an outward–focused, self-forgetful life of love. We cannot. The hole inside us is too big, our emptiness and fears too great. But when we know we are deeply and forever loved, as we become increasingly secure in that love, then love begets love. Real freedom is a life of overflowing, undefeatable love. God meets our greatest need with his undeserved love—and only then, in the security of that undeserved love, he calls us into his eternal dance of love:

> To run and do the Law commands
> But it gives me neither feet nor hands!
> Better news the gospel brings
> It bids me fly, and it gives me wings!
> Dive in and learn to fly. . .

A final word: the quality of any "theological" work—any book about God—can be gauged by whether it leaves us more in love with the God revealed in Jesus Christ, or mainly impressed by the author's ability to write well.

Truth be told, for three decades Dr. Clay Peck *has* impressed me as a thoughtful scholar, a healthy, dedicated pastor of a thriving congregation, and a very cherished friend. But diving into Clay's walk through the apostle Paul's letter to the Galatians, very quickly Clay and even Paul were out of sight. I was again caught up in the depth and beauty of what God has given us in Christ, and why he, Jesus, is worth living and dying for. That became truer with each page turned on this 40-day journey (which I devoured in four). Give yourself the gift of this journey.

PREFACE

Scottish freedom fighter William Wallace attempts to motivate his beleaguered and outnumbered troops to rally against their British oppressors in the blockbuster movie *Braveheart*. With war paint on his face, pacing back and forth on his spirited battle horse, the mighty warrior of freedom loudly and authoritatively declares:

> *Aye, fight, and you may die. Run, and you'll live. . . at least a while. And dying in your beds, many years from now, would you be willin' to trade all the days, from this day to that, for one chance, just one chance, to come back here and tell our enemies that they may take our lives, but they'll never take. . . our freedom?*

I love that scene, which reminds me of the longing in each person's heart—the longing for freedom. Freedom is worth fighting for, and once you attain it, you do not want to lose it. That is what this book is about—finding freedom and protecting it.

Growing up in a rules–oriented, legalistic, fundamentalist church, I became discouraged with religion as a young person, believing that I could never live up to all the written and unwritten requirements and expectations. Abandoning religion entirely, I lived a reckless lifestyle, rebelling against God, my parents, my teachers, and all authority. I wanted to be free. However, I discovered that a self–centered life does not bring freedom, rather just another form of bondage. Over time, I learned there are two different ditches that rob people of joy—legalism or license, the law or the flesh. The enemy of my soul did not care which ditch I chose as long as he could steer me off the center pathway—the gospel pathway, the path to freedom.

In this book you will find daily devotional readings that will help you experience the type of true freedom Jesus promised when he said, "if the Son sets you free, you will be free indeed" (John 8:36). Whether you breeze straight through this book, or read it slowly, day by day, I hope and pray you will take the time to meditate on the concepts and apply them to your life. I hope this journey through the apostle Paul's New Testament epistle to the Galatians will remind you the gospel of grace in Christ Jesus not only sets you free but keeps you free, as long as you determine to keep it the *main thing*.

DAY 1

WHAT IS YOUR MAIN THING?

O n my right forearm is a tattoo that reads "The Main Thing is to Keep the Main Thing the Main Thing." When I first rolled up my sleeve to reveal the tattoo during an Easter service at Grace Place, I told the church I had thought about it for a long time and decided to get the tattoo for two reasons.

The secondary reason was that I was tired of judgmental Christians. I had heard people say negative things about tattoos and was embarrassed by that. My son has tattoos on his arms, and he told me he wore long sleeves around certain people for fear they would judge him. Really? I do not think Jesus judged anyone for how they looked. I do not want to be—or be perceived as—a judgmental religious person, so I decided I would remove all doubt about whether people with tattoos are welcome at my church. I also made a joke and told all the parents if they were worried about the pastor being a bad influence, they could tell their kids they could have one too if they waited, like the pastor, until they were fifty years old!

1

But, more importantly, the primary reason I got that tattoo was because I wanted to permanently declare what is most important to me. I am not suggesting you need to get a tattoo in order to witness, but my tattoo has opened the door for me to share my faith many times. When people see that tattoo and ask me what the "main thing" is, I point to my other tattoo on my left arm—a cross made up of three nails tied together. I tell them that for me the main thing is the cross of Christ, and these nails remind me that he took those nails for me—they were my nails. If they want to know more, I talk to them about the difference between religion (spelled "D-O") and the gospel (spelled "D-O-N-E").

The cross of Christ is the main thing; it is of first importance. Notice the theme sounded over and over throughout the New Testament:

> May I never boast except in the cross of our Lord Jesus Christ, through which the world has been crucified to me, and I to the world. (Galatians 6:14)

> For the message of the cross is foolishness to those who are perishing, but to us who are being saved it is the power of God. (1 Corinthians 1:18)

> For I resolved to know nothing while I was with you except Jesus Christ and him crucified. (1 Corinthians 2:2)

> For what I received I passed on to you as of first importance: that Christ died for our sins according to the Scriptures, that he was buried, that he was raised on the third day according to the Scriptures. (1 Corinthians 15:3–4)

Christianity is not a philosophy; it is a person, it is Jesus, and it is centered in what he did for humanity on Easter weekend—it is the cross and the resurrection. This is the message of the gospel, the good news.

Notice that above all else this message is *of first importance.* That means if we make a list—however long—of important or non-important things the simple gospel message is of first importance.

The number–one core value at Grace Place, the church I planted and am privileged to lead, is "The Main Thing is to Keep the Main Thing the Main Thing." I repeated that value three times in my very first sermon on September 14, 1996 in the rented Berthoud High School auditorium, and I have been repeating it ever since.

Why am I so passionate about the keeping the main thing the main thing? Growing up in a fundamentalist religious system that was all about rules, rules, and more rules, the list long, the rules both written and unwritten. We believed in Jesus, but. . . There was always a big but. "But you must do this, and this, and this to be saved or to stay saved." It was a "Christ–plus–something–gospel," which, as we will see as we get into verse–by–verse reflection of the New Testament epistle of Galatians, is really no gospel at all.

Over time I have noticed some believers and churches have no main thing. They may believe many things, but it is not clear what is central. There is just a bunch of stuff to know and believe but no clarity. There is no central thing worth fighting for, living for—even dying for.

Then there are some who make everything the main thing. You better know everything on the belief list (every do and every don't) because it is all equally important, and if you are not in line with it, you do not belong. These people have a long list of beliefs and practices one must agree to (in every detail) in order to be accepted in the group, and they are all of equal importance. Rejecting one point means you are not living up to the truth and might as well have rejected the whole package. Some form of the gospel may be hidden in there somewhere, but it is not supreme—it is just one more of numerous other essentials.

Others have the wrong main thing, something other than the gospel. I do not think any believer or church will say something other than Jesus and the cross is central. But if you listen to them long enough, you soon can hear some special teaching other than the gospel emphasized above all others—perhaps a particular doctrine that makes that group distinctive.

If you ever find yourself in a church or denomination that has no main thing, or appears to make everything the main thing, or focuses on the wrong main thing, *get out!* Find a healthy church committed to keeping the gospel the main thing. There are plenty of biblical doctrinal beliefs sincere believers will disagree on. And that is okay as long as there is unity on the main thing. We can agree to disagree (hopefully without being disagreeable) on secondary doctrinal issues. Exhorting the church to accept each other without "quarrelling over disputable matters" (Romans 14:1), the apostle Paul encourages believers to keep our focus on what is most important.

A healthy believer or church will keep the gospel as the main thing—the good news that a loving God has taken the initiative to do for us what we could never do for ourselves, offering us the gift of salvation by grace alone, through faith alone, based on Christ's perfect, finished work alone. Plus nothing. Period.

During these forty short chapters, or forty days of devotional reading if you so choose, I invite you to consider what your main thing is and how you are keeping the main thing the main thing.

REFLECTION

When have I confused the "main thing" with something else?

In what ways am I keeping the "main thing" central in my life? In what ways am I losing sight of it?

DAY 2

LAW PLACE OR GRACE PLACE?

I have the privilege of being the founding pastor of Grace Place in Berthoud, Colorado. While driving to Colorado from Maryland with my family and all my belongings, I was thinking and praying about the church I planned to start and what to call it. God's grace had become a precious reality in my life, and I wanted to use the word grace in the church name. With so many "Grace Community" or "Grace Fellowship" churches out there, I wanted something unique. One night we parked across the street from a church called Christ Place. Immediately I had it: Grace Place!

Grace Place is very intentionally named because I came from "law place." Growing up in a fundamentalist denomination focused on rule keeping, I got turned off to religion as a teenager and rebelled. After a few years of foolishness, living for myself and the world, I decided I wanted to follow Jesus, but it took me a number of years to come to understand the difference between the Old Covenant and the New Covenant and to get clarity on the essence and centrality of the gospel.

During my twenties, I went through what I like to call a personal "grace awakening." I studied and preached through Galatians, Romans, Ephesians, and other New Testament passages. As an associate pastor under Dr. Richard Fredericks, he recommended I read John Stott's seminal masterpiece *The Cross of Christ,* and helped me significantly to establish the gospel as the main thing in my life and teaching.

I read *The Purpose Driven Church* by Rick Warren the year it came out in 1995. In the preface, Warren writes about when he first experienced a call to plant a church and his first member, along with his wife, was the realtor who helped him find a place to live when he moved to Orange County, California. That story lit a fire in my heart to also start a church and build it from the foundation up over the long haul. I highlighted a text in my Bible where Paul says, "It has always been my ambition to preach the gospel where Christ was not known, so that I would not be building on someone else's foundation" (Romans 15:20).

I told the Lord I felt called to plant a church. If the Lord would allow me to plant a church in Colorado where I grew up and longed to return, it would be a huge bonus, one I would be extremely grateful for. Not long after, I received a surprise phone call from someone I did not know, inviting me to come out and consult with a handful of families who were interested in starting a new church in northern Colorado. God gave me the desire of my heart.

At our first worship service, in a rented high school auditorium, I preached about the type of church God was calling Grace Place to be. Three times in that message I repeated, and asked the brand-new congregation to repeat with me, *The Main Thing is to Keep the Main Thing the Main Thing.* That statement, which I have reiterated like a broken record ever since, long before branding it on my arm, has helped to build a welcoming, accepting, united, joyous, and generous culture in our congregation.

During the difficult pandemic year of 2020 many churches divided and were consumed with argument and anger—anger over how to respond to the COVID virus, whether to close the doors, when to reopen, how to relate to restrictions, how to respond appropriately to racial tensions, how to navigate a contentious political election, etc. I heard stories from other pastors about people leaving and writing hateful messages on social media platforms. That did not happen at Grace Place. I really believe one reason we stayed united was because of the culture that has been intentionally developed around keeping the main thing the main thing. Our people know and believe we can agree to disagree on secondary issues but stay united around the gospel. Theology impacts culture and behavior.

In the pages ahead I want to walk you through Paul's epistle to the Galatians. I encourage you to read this book with an open Bible. You will get more out of it if you look closely at the context and wording in the text. Sometimes Paul's arguments are dense. You will have to be willing to put on your thinking cap in spots, but I believe you will be blessed by that effort.

We might consider Galatians a premier epistle. Next to Romans, which is a longer and more systematic presentation, Galatians is the foremost gospel epistle in all Scripture. I hope and pray and believe God will speak to you very deeply and personally as we journey together. I pray also that some people will get set free from sin and come to faith in Jesus; others will be set free from legalistic bondage and religion gone bad and find new joy and freedom; and still others will grow in their walk with Jesus and appreciate the gospel like never before.

Consider me your tour guide! For years, my wife, a high school teacher, and I have led educational tours in the summer. We always have a local tour director who meets us at the airport, then local guides meet us at each major stop. They bring to life the history and culture of the country they live in.

While I will be a reliable guide and point things out as we travel through Galatians together, I am praying the Word of God will impact you and change your life. Most of the blessing you receive will be from your own observation and individual enlightenment from the Holy Spirit.

> For the word of God is alive and active. Sharper than any double–edged sword, it penetrates even to dividing soul and spirit, joints and marrow; it judges the thoughts and attitudes of the heart. (Hebrews 4:12)

REFLECTION

What has been my understanding of law and grace?

Growing up, was my life impacted more by law or grace? In what ways?

DAY 3

A LIBERATION
LETTER

The good news presented in Galatians is summarized in this key verse: "It is for freedom that Christ has set us free. Stand firm, then, and do not let yourselves be burdened again by a yoke of slavery" (Galatians 5:1).

Galatians has been called the "charter of Christian freedom," "the Magna Carta of spiritual liberty," "the battle cry of the Reformation," and the "Christian's declaration of independence." Martin Luther's commentary on Galatians laid the foundation for the Protestant Reformation. In Galatians and Romans, Luther discovered the pure gospel of grace, which was contrary to the salvation–by–works teaching that had evolved in the Roman Catholic Church. Luther once said: "The epistle to the Galatians is my epistle. To it I am, as it were, in wedlock. Galatians is my Katherine" (Luther's wife's name).[1]

In order to properly understand Galatians, it is important to consider the *setting* in which this book was written and the *problem* to which it responds.

First, the *setting*. Galatians was the first letter the apostle Paul wrote. At one time Paul had been an opponent of Christianity, and as a strict Jewish Pharisee, he not only rejected Christ, he gave all his energy toward stamping out Christianity, considering it a dangerous heresy with potential to undermine the Jewish law and practice. But then Paul met the living, resurrected Christ on the road to Damascus, and after that encounter, Paul would never be the same again. He dedicated the rest of his life to telling others about the risen Christ.

During the course of his ministry, Paul went on three major missionary trips, preaching the gospel and establishing churches. The first missionary trip is described in Acts 13–14. Paul and his buddy Barnabas left their home base in Antioch and traveled through the southern region of Galatia (modern–day Turkey). They preached in such cities as Antioch of Pisidia, Iconium, Lystra, and Derbe. Acts 13:49 reports: "The word of the Lord spread through the whole region." On their return trip they stopped in all the places they had established congregations, strengthening the believers, appointing pastors (Acts 14:21–23).

Sometime after returning to their home base in Antioch, Paul got news that false teachers had followed behind him perverting the gospel: "Certain people came down from Judea to Antioch and were teaching the believers: 'Unless you are circumcised, according to the custom taught by Moses, you cannot be saved'" (Acts 15:1).

These false teachers were known as Judaizers. They accepted Christ was the Messiah, but they insisted new converts must also obey the law of Moses with all its regulations in order to be saved. They were false teachers because they were distorting the gospel. They were preaching a gospel of "Jesus *plus* something."

This is the *problem* that occasioned the book of Galatians. Hearing that the new converts throughout the region of Galatia were becoming confused and slipping into legalistic bondage, Paul was moved by the

Holy Spirit to write a letter filled with passion—*a liberation letter*. This earlier Christian controversy was not a gentle one. Acts 15:2 speaks of "sharp dispute and debate." Some things are worth fighting for; the gospel is one of them.

The problem became so severe that the famous Jerusalem Council was convened where it was concluded the new Gentile converts would *not* be subjected to the law of Moses as New Covenant Christians. The Jerusalem Council (Acts 15) probably happened around the year 49 AD. Written sometime between the events of Acts 14 and 15, the book of Galatians was written *after* Paul's first missionary trip and *before* the Jerusalem Council. No doubt he would have mentioned the decision of the elders and apostles in the letter if it had been written after the Jerusalem Council. A number of scholars put the date of Galatians at 48 AD, which makes it one of the earliest New Testament books written— definitely Paul's first.

There were two issues Paul had to combat in his letter:

- **First, the false teachers attacked his credibility.** They went to the new churches and said Paul could not be trusted. He was not an official representative of the church. He was not a true apostle—one of the original twelve. He had no authority. Because of these kinds of allegations, Paul had to spend the first two chapters of Galatians defending his apostolic calling.

- **Second, the Judaizers insisted Paul's gospel was wrong.** "Jesus only" was not enough. Yes, Jesus was the Messiah, sent from God, but there was more. The Gentiles needed to accept the Old Covenant law—in essence they needed to become Jewish Christians, and the new converts must become circumcised.

Reading through Galatians it seems like "circumcision" was the main issue with these Judaizers. In fact, Paul called them "the circumcision group" (Galatians 2:12). But circumcision was not the real issue. The issue was the law of Moses. Circumcision was just the entry sign into the covenant (Genesis 17:11), a catchword for the whole system. You must keep this in mind as we progress through Galatians in order to get the full meaning. Let me illustrate with two verses:

> Then some of the believers who belonged to the party of the Pharisees stood up and said, "The Gentiles must be circumcised and required to keep the law of Moses." (Acts 15:5)

> Again I declare to every man who lets himself be circumcised that he is obligated to obey the whole law. (Galatians 5:3)

The Judaizers were preaching a distorted gospel, saying Christ plus allegiance to the law of Moses was necessary for salvation. (As we will see in the next chapter, a Christ–plus–something gospel is really no gospel at all!)

As you read and study Galatians, keep in mind that the issues discussed were more than just theological. They were also social and cultural and were all tied up together. It was hard for some of the Jewish Christians to accept this new concept of Gentiles being welcomed into the family of God. Keep in mind that not only did strict Jews avoid contact with Gentiles, they had sayings such as: "The best of snakes, crush; the best of the Gentiles, kill," and "God created the Gentiles to be fuel for the fires of Hell." They even crafted a law that made it illegal to help a Gentile mother in her most desperate hour, for that would only bring another Gentile into the world.

Coming from that mindset, thinking they were the only chosen ones, it was very difficult for some of the Jewish Christians to accept the new Gentile converts. When they reluctantly gave in to the notion of Gentile Christians, they decided they could allow the Gentiles into their world, but only if they became Jewish-like. So, as you read Galatians you will notice an emphasis on the outward, defining boundary markers. Issues that were not only theological but also cultural—especially circumcision. Food laws (Galatians 2:12) and Jewish holy days (Galatians 4:10) were issues as well. All of these were important issues to the Jews because they separated them from the rest of the world and defined who was in the community.

REFLECTION

What boundary markers have I experienced that kept me inside or outside of a group?

When have I imposed boundary markers on myself or others? Have they been biblical or cultural? Have they resulted in liberation or bondage?

DAY 4

GRACE AND PEACE

A t first glance things like circumcision, food laws, and holy days
seem to have nothing to do with the issues we face, but the
book of Galatians is extremely relevant to us today because
the fundamental issue was a gospel of *Jesus only* versus a gospel of *Jesus
plus something*. That continues to be a debate in every generation even
though the plus–something issues may change.

There is nothing wrong with circumcision. It is commonly
practiced in our country today—*but not as a religious obligation*. There
is nothing wrong with following some kind of diet restrictions—your
doctor may even instruct you for health reasons to cut back or eliminate
some food—*but not as a religious obligation*. There is nothing wrong with
observing some day on the calendar—*but not as a religious obligation*.

There are many issues people over time have tried to tack on to the
gospel as salvation issues. Watch out for it because it is a distortion of the
gospel and happens quite regularly.

In the 1970s Paul Hiebert, a missiologist and cultural
anthropologist, questioned how much of the gospel message an illiterate
and impoverished person in a non-western context must understand in

order to be a Christian. What if they could not read the Bible or only heard about Jesus once? How could you know if they were God's children or not? Of course, only God knows the heart, but what indicators might there be?[2]

Using "set theory" (a type of mathematics), Hiebert proposed a new paradigm, contrasting a "bounded set" or a "centered set" model.

- **Bounded Set**: This type is *static*—it is all about boundaries. Those in fellowship with God affirm right beliefs and practice right behaviors. Those who do not are not in fellowship with God. You are in or out based on the boundary.
- **Centered Set**: This type is *dynamic*—it is all about movement in a particular direction. Those in fellowship with God are moving toward Jesus rather than away from him.[3]

This can be applied to churches. Some churches are all about the *boundaries*—defining who is in and who is out. This leads to pride and judgmentalism, and it turns a lot of people off.

Healthy churches are all about Jesus—moving toward him is the goal. One of our core values at Grace Place is you can "Belong Before you Believe." If people hang out with Jesus and his followers long enough, they are likely to believe in him eventually. Jesus said, "I, when I am lifted up from the earth, will draw all people to myself" (John 12:32).

In the wide–open outback of Australia there are two main methods for keeping cattle on the ranch. One is to build a fence around the perimeter; the other is to dig a well in the center of the property. Do you agree with me that Jesus is more like a well than a fence?

The problem facing the Galatian churches was that the Judaizers were all about the traditional boundaries of the Jewish law. With that background regarding the setting and problem, let us look at the introduction—just five verses:

Paul, an apostle—sent not from men nor by a man, but by
Jesus Christ and God the Father, who raised him from the
dead—and all the brothers and sisters with me,

To the churches in Galatia:

Grace and peace to you from God our Father and the Lord
Jesus Christ, who gave himself for our sins to rescue us from the
present evil age, according to the will of our God and Father,
to whom be glory for ever and ever. Amen. (Galatians 1:1–5)

Paul always starts his letters with a standardized approach: 1)
identification of the writer ; 2) identification of the recipient(s); 3) a
greeting. Paul follows that custom in all his letters. But he modifies it,
too. In Paul's letters he usually includes a brief kernel of what the whole
letter is about in his introduction. In this case he is planning to defend
his authority as an apostle and then present the gospel, which sets us free
in Christ. Notice how these two themes are introduced right here in the
introduction.

First, he introduces himself as *Paul, an apostle.* By starting the letter
this way Paul is not bragging; rather he is establishing his credibility
from the start. He will have more to say about his unique, divine calling,
but right up front he wants the listener to take note that this is an apostle
speaking.

An *apostle* in New Testament times was one of a small group who
had witnessed the resurrected Christ and been specifically commissioned
by him as a unique ambassador. They represented Jesus and spoke his
word with authority. God ordained them to found the church, and the
Holy Spirit used several of them to write the New Covenant Word of
God—the New Testament Scriptures. In that sense there are no apostles
today; apostles fulfilled a first century role whereby Christ laid the
foundation for his church.

Obviously, it was a serious thing for Paul to lay claim to such a title, and, not surprisingly, the Judaizers challenged his credibility. Maybe they referenced the fact that Paul had not been one of the original twelve called by Jesus.

Paul insists his calling was genuine, though unique. He had been appointed by the resurrected Christ, although later than the other apostles. He stresses he was *sent not from men nor by a man but by Jesus Christ and God the Father who raised him from the dead.* These are words to take seriously, both for the original listeners and for you and me. For if Paul was truly an appointed apostle or representative for the risen Christ and the Father God, then we had better listen to what he says. Jesus told his apostles: "Anyone who welcomes you welcomes me, and anyone who receives me welcomes the one who sent me" (Matthew 10:40). We are carefully studying these words and willing to submit our lives to whatever they say because we believe they are Christ's words to us through his chosen apostle.

The second theme introduced in the introduction is the precious *gospel* which was the passion of Paul's life and ministry. "Grace and peace to you" (Galatians 1:3). The Hebrews used peace as a greeting—*shalom.* The Greeks used grace as a greeting—*charis.* Paul combines them and infuses deep theological meaning into them by adding "from God our Father and the Lord Jesus Christ" (Galatians 1:3).

Paul always utilizes them in this order at the beginning of his letters—*Grace and peace.* This is profoundly significant.

- **Grace** is God's free and unmerited favor, which he bestows on us in Christ. He saves us quite apart from anything we can contribute, for salvation is a free gift—by grace alone. Grace is the *root* of our salvation.
- **Peace** is the *fruit* of our salvation. It is the result of grace accepted and experienced, it is reconciliation—peace with God, peace with each other, peace with our own conscience.

It's a beautiful greeting, rich with meaning. God's grace produces peace, and it was revealed at Calvary's cross in Christ, "who gave himself for our sins to rescue us from the present evil age, according to the will of our God and Father" (Galatians 1:4).

This verse tells us three things about the cross. At the cross:

1) Jesus gave himself for our sins. Jesus Christ willingly bore the curse for sin. He took the judgment our sins deserved and offered himself as a sin-offering. He did not give gold or silver or lambs or bulls—or even angels. He gave the ultimate gift—he gave himself.

Why? *For our sins.* Please be assured that you are included in the unifying and inclusive pronoun "*our.*" It was for your sin and mine and every human being that Jesus suffered and provided atonement. Christ did not just die for the best of us—he died for the worst of us. He did not die for just the big sins—he also died for the small ones. He did not die for a few sins—he died for every and all sin.

Do you believe Jesus died for you personally? Many of us do. We love the Lord and know he has forgiven us. But sometimes we feel like failures, like our sins are too great. That is when we need to remind ourselves of the good news that Jesus *gave himself for our sins.* He took them—all of them—and dealt with them once and for all. At the cross, Jesus gave himself for our sins.

2) Jesus rescued us from the present evil age. Here is the keynote of Galatians. We have been delivered, rescued, and set free in Christ. Christianity is a rescue religion. The Bible divides history into two ages: "this age" and "the age to come." The New Testament teaches that Christ has already inaugurated the age to come.

The two ages are now running parallel. They overlap between the cross and the Second Coming of Jesus. When we are converted, we are transferred into the new age. As followers of Christ we began to live the new life of the age to come, even now. So, Christ's death provides not only the forgiveness of sins, but the opportunity to live a new life—

the life of the age to come. Through the cross we are rescued from this present evil age. Already.

3) Jesus died according to the will of our God and Father. Your Father in heaven loves you. He wants you saved. It is his will and desire; he is for you! I hope you have (or had) a good father in this life. I hope if you are a dad, you are modeling loving fatherhood to your child, but no matter how good a father you are, no matter how wonderful a father you have (or had), no earthly father can compare to the Father in heaven who has poured out all heaven in order to draw you to himself and save you for eternity. The cross was his will because he loves you and knew it was the only way for the curse of sin to be broken.

Paul packed a lot into these opening verses, so it is no wonder that even after his mini gospel summary he cannot go on without bursting into a short doxology: "to whom be glory for ever and ever. Amen" (Galatians 1:5).

REFLECTION

Has the church been a place where I can "belong before I believe?" How so?

Am I involved in a healthy church that is focused on Jesus and the goal of knowing him better? What outward signs indicate my church is healthy or unhealthy?

DAY 5

FREEDOM
IS WORTH
FIGHTING FOR

I am sure you will agree some things are worth fighting for. On my short list of things really worth fighting for is *freedom*. If you try to mess with my family, watch out, I am ready to fight to protect them, because their freedom matters greatly to me! If a person, or a group of people, or a nation, is oppressed, it is worth fighting to gain or preserve those freedoms. In the church as well, freedom is worth fighting for, and the good news of freedom in Christ, the liberating gospel of grace, must be protected and defended.

A lot of issues Christians fight about are really not worthy of a fight. I find it helpful to draw three circles, like a target, to illustrate the priority of the gospel.

1) In the small, center circle is the New Testament gospel—the bull's-eye. The gospel is the main thing. It is proclaimed in the infallible Word of God, the Bible. It is the good news that a loving God has taken

21

the initiative to save unworthy sinners by grace only, through faith only, by Christ's cross only—totally apart from any of our good works and in spite of our bad deeds.

2) The next circle represents important, yet secondary issues—church doctrines and positions. In this category believers should study the Bible and know what they believe but not fight and argue and divide the church. A long list of examples could include the method of baptism, the age of the world, eschatology (last day events), Calvinism versus Arminianism, the place of miraculous spiritual gifts in the church, the role of women in ministry, church governance style, etc. When it comes to secondary issues, it is advantageous to study, discuss, and debate, but unworthy to fight.

3) The outer circle represents lifestyle issues where the Bible is silent, and individual believers come to different conclusions and need to respect each other's choices. Again, a long list could be made: whether or not a Christian should go to movies, dance, send children to public school, let their kids trick or treat, wear a suit or jeans to church, styles of worship music, how often to observe the Lord's Supper, and the list goes on.

These issues are not worth fighting over. Know what you believe and why and then live it, but do not try and force your lifestyle choices on others; let the Holy Spirit lead and do his job to direct. Paul wrote we are not to quarrel over "disputable matters" (Romans 14:1) and to not judge people who exercise their Christian liberty differently from us (Romans 14:13). The ancient motto of the church (often attributed to Augustine) is most helpful: "In essentials, unity; in non-essentials, liberty; in all things, charity."

Unfortunately, churches and church groups have often expanded the inner circle. Many churches include lots of secondary issues in the first circle, resulting in no main thing or multiple main things, which only muddies the supremacy and centrality of the pure and simple New

Testament gospel, leading to skirmishes and fighting over secondary issues, and ultimately resulting in divisions within the Body of Christ.

Other groups, such as fundamentalist types, have drawn the first circle to include everything in the third circle as well, according to their own unique definitions, of course. This results in legalism and heresy because everything becomes a salvation issue and a way to determine who is inside the elite group and who is outside.

And then a sad thing happens. Young people who grow up in that kind of system often get discouraged because they cannot keep all the rules or do not feel they need to. Instead of picking and choosing for themselves based on their own Bible study and walk with God, they often just give up on the whole business. If they cannot measure up in one area, they might as well let it all go since it is all of equal importance, a package deal. Tragically, this is why they have never understood the difference between Jesus and religion, so, they just chuck it all. This is so heartbreaking because many of these young people (and older people too) who think they have given up on Christ and Christianity have really given up on *fundamentalist religion.* If only they clearly understood the beauty and centrality of Jesus and his gospel, the gospel that draws and secures the lost through inexorable love, they may not have left.

What I want to say clearly is there is only one gospel, it is of first importance, and it is *worth fighting for!* Many, many things are not worth fighting for, but the gospel is. The gospel is the main thing upon which the Church is built, and if the gospel is altered, distorted, or changed, the foundation is knocked out from under the church, and the whole thing collapses into a meaningless system of ritual and bondage.

REFLECTION

What arguments over secondary or lifestyle issues have I experienced in the church?

Have I ever had to fight for the gospel? If not, would I be willing to fight for it?

THERE IS ONLY
ONE GOSPEL

Consistently, in all of Paul's epistles, after the greeting he continues for a number of verses with a prayer or statement of thanksgiving for those to whom he is writing. Often, he mentions their faith and perseverance, but Galatians is the only letter where he launches into a rebuke without first giving thanks for something commendable about the churches he is addressing. Messing with the gospel is serious business. The gospel is worth fighting for, and so Paul does. His militant tone seeps through in these verses:

> I am astonished that you are so quickly deserting the one who called you to live in the grace of Christ and are turning to a different gospel—which is really no gospel at all. Evidently some people are throwing you into confusion and are trying to pervert the gospel of Christ. But even if we or an angel from heaven should preach a gospel other than the one we preached to you, let them be under God's curse! As we have

already said, so now I say again: If anybody is preaching to you a gospel other than what you accepted, let them be under God's curse! Am I now trying to win the approval of human beings, or of God? Or am I trying to please people? If I were still trying to please people, I would not be a servant of Christ. (Galatians 1:6–10)

I imagine Paul striding back and forth dictating this letter under the inspiration of the Holy Spirit, his brow creased, his fists clenched, and his veins bulging. This passionate fighting language is not of a selfishly jealous man throwing a temper tantrum, blowing off steam, it is godly zeal for what matters most. Paul is protective of two treasures that are being threatened—the pure gospel of grace, and the precious new converts who have freshly accepted the gospel.

In these verses I hear Paul sounding both a *warning* and an *appeal*. Here is the message in a nutshell: There is only one gospel, so do not desert it or distort it, but rather discern it and defend it!

THERE IS ONLY ONE GOSPEL

Paul says if you turn to a different gospel it is *really no gospel at all.* People present a variety of theologies under the heading of "the gospel." Most every church group—even cult groups—say they are preaching the gospel. In fact, they will often call their attempts to convert others to their unique perspective as "taking the gospel to the world." But there is only one gospel, and any other version is a perversion. His implied warning is twofold: do not desert (as the Galatians were doing); and do not distort (as the Judaizers were doing).

DO NOT DESERT THE GOSPEL

"I am astonished that you are so quickly deserting the one who called you to live in the grace of Christ and are turning to a different gospel" (Galatians 1:6). Paul expresses his wonder and amazement that the new converts who recently accepted the gospel are already turning from it. The language, "so quickly," indicates it has not been long since he was with them. The word *desert* in the Greek is a term used to describe military defectors, soldiers who go over to the other side, turncoats. It does not indicate a slight change but a total turnaround. It is a far worse betrayal than abandoning our cherished political party or football team. Paul states if you turn to a so–called different gospel, you are really deserting the one who called you by the grace of Christ. To accept a version of the gospel other than the one presented by the apostles is actually to desert the Lord. This is serious business.

Paul defines in brief what the gospel is back in verse 4. According to that summary, the gospel is all about Jesus and what he has already done for us. It is not about us and what we need to do; it is about Jesus. So, if we turn away from it to some other kind of teaching that attaches human works and requirements for salvation, we are not just turning away from the gospel message, we are turning away from Jesus himself, who is the heart and essence of the gospel message.

Paul's first warning is not to desert. Temptations to give in to a so–called gospel that includes humans in the equation will constantly exist because the flesh always wants recognition. All other religions (and all perversions of Christianity) are about *humans* doing something. Christianity is about *God* doing something. Do not desert. The second warning here is:

DO NOT DISTORT THE GOSPEL

"Not that there is another one, but there are some who trouble you and want to distort the gospel of Christ (Galatians 1:7 ESV). Here is the first mention of the "Judaizers" who were troubling the new converts and throwing them into confusion, false teachers who were distorting the gospel by adding to it. One of my favorite commentators, John Stott, wrote this concerning the false teachers:

They did not deny that you must believe in Jesus for salvation, but they stressed that you must be circumcised and keep the law as well. In other words, you must let Moses finish what Christ has begun. Or rather, you yourself must finish, by your obedience to the law, what Christ has begun. You must add your works to the work of Christ. You must finish Christ's unfinished work.[4]

Can you see how this was heresy? The gospel is all about Christ's finished work by grace alone, through faith alone, plus nothing, period. But these false teachers were saying, "No, it is not finished. It has just started. It is not by grace alone plus nothing, it is by grace plus something—plus the law." But a Christ–plus–something gospel is no gospel at all—it is a distortion.

In verse 7, the verb *pervert* in the NIV is translated *distort* in the ESV. It comes from a Greek word which means "to reverse." You see, you cannot modify the gospel without completely changing it. If you add works, it is not the gospel anymore!

Listen to this clear message trumpeted throughout the New Testament:

> For it is by grace you have been saved, through faith—and this is not from yourselves, it is the gift of God—not by works, so that no one can boast. (Ephesians 2:8–9)

> He has saved us and called us to a holy life—not because of anything we have done but because of his own purpose and grace. This grace was given us in Christ Jesus before the beginning of time. . . (2 Timothy 1:9)

> He saved us, not because of righteous things we had done, but because of his mercy. . . (Titus 3:5)

Human works play no part in salvation. Good works are a response to salvation, the fruit, not the root. Believers are working *from* victory not *toward* victory.

REFLECTION

When have I deserted or distorted the gospel, and how do/did I correct that?

What does the phrase "working from victory not toward victory" mean to me?

DAY 7

DISCERN AND DEFEND THE GOSPEL

In Galatians 1, Paul emphatically asserts there is only one gospel, and, he warns not to desert or distort it. Instead, his implied encouragement is for us to discern and defend the one true gospel.

DISCERN THE GOSPEL

"But even if we or an angel from heaven should preach a gospel other than the one we preached to you, let them be under God's curse" (Galatians 1:8). This is serious business. Paul pronounces a curse on anyone who preaches another version of the gospel, even himself or an angel from heaven. Obviously, a true angel or a true apostle would not distort the gospel, but Paul wants his readers to understand the necessity of discernment. The messenger must be judged by the message, not the other way around. Do not think just because a person is eloquent, educated, well-known, or popular that whatever they say is truth. In another place, Paul warns against false teachers:

> For such people are false apostles, deceitful workers, masquerading as apostles of Christ. And no wonder, for Satan himself masquerades as an angel of light. It is not surprising, then, if his servants also masquerade as servants of righteousness. Their end will be what their actions deserve. (2 Corinthians 11:13–15)

It takes discernment to determine and hold fast to the true gospel. Do not modify your view of the gospel based on what spokespersons say, instead, modify your opinion of spokespersons based on how they square with the gospel. Throughout history so–called prophets have claimed they got revelations from angels or visions and then went on to write things that contradicted the gospel of grace alone. So, beware. Exercise discernment. If you are reading a book or listening to a TV or radio preacher, or a podcast or YouTube video, or the pastor of your church, how can you discern if the gospel being preached is true?

Consider two things: substance and source. Consider first the *substance*. The gospel is a gospel of grace, that is, free, unmerited favor with God through Christ alone. Whenever someone starts adding to it, he or she is corrupting it. That is the first test.

Consider, second, the *source*. Check the origin of the gospel. The source of the true gospel is the message authoritatively preached by the apostles commissioned by Christ and is now recorded in the New Testament. Paul says that even he or an angel could not alter what he had originally presented because it was not "his" message. Directly commissioned and instructed by the risen Lord Jesus and appointed to present the gospel in a format that would become the written and preserved Word of God, Paul relentlessly proclaimed the pure gospel.

Peter once said that when the Holy Spirit moved on the prophets and apostles resulting in the written Word, it became more reliable than an eyewitness report (2 Peter 1:19).

Discern the true gospel by considering the *substance* (is it a message of free grace?) and the *source* (is it rooted and grounded in the plain teaching of the New Testament?). Along with a clear warning not to desert or distort the gospel, I hear an implied appeal in Galatians 1 for believers to be able to discern the gospel and be willing (if necessary) to defend the gospel.

DEFEND THE GOSPEL

"As we have already said, so now I say again: If anybody is preaching to you a gospel other than what you accepted, let them be under God's curse" (Galatians 1:9). To underscore the importance of what he has just said in verse 8, Paul repeats it in verse 9, changing it slightly. In verse 8, he speaks of the gospel that had been preached. In verse 9 he calls it the gospel you accepted. Instead of saying "we preached" the true gospel (and someone else distorted it), he now puts some of the responsibility onto them and says, "You accepted it." It is as though he is saying, "Yes, the false teachers bear responsibility for this distortion and are in fact deserving of condemnation, but you Galatians bear some responsibility too. You understood and embraced the message of grace. You accepted it!"

Every believer has a responsibility to hang onto the gospel once accepted and defend it if necessary. Paul certainly provides a model for us here. In his defense of the gospel he employs some pretty strong language. Twice he pronounces a curse on false teachers saying: *Let him be eternally condemned.* These are sobering words! The Greek word is *anathema*, which means to be under the curse of God, devoted to destruction. At first glance that seems a little extreme. "Come on, Paul, you are defending the gospel of grace, but that does not sound very gracious," we want to say.

Paul was not speaking idly, rashly, off the cuff, or out of uncontrolled temper. The text makes that clear. Notice two things:

- First, he was *impartial*. He included himself potentially in the curse. This conveys he was not just lashing out against enemies.
- Second, he was very *deliberate* in his curse, repeating it again for emphasis.

So why would Paul, under the inspiration of the Holy Spirit, speak so harshly regarding those who preach a distorted gospel? I believe Paul has three reasons for defending the gospel with such aggression. Three critical issues were at stake in Paul's mind: the sufficiency of the cross, the stability of the church, and the approval of God.

THE SUFFICIENCY OF THE CROSS

The false teachers were implying Christ's work was not finished or complete, ultimately making the work of Christ insufficient. Imagine the cross insufficient to save mankind, necessitating human achievements or accomplishments to attain salvation. That line of reasoning would eventually make the cross not just insufficient, but unnecessary. Later Paul states, "I do not set aside the grace of God, for if righteousness could be gained through the law, Christ died for nothing" (Galatians 2:21). The sufficiency of the cross was at stake.

THE STABILITY OF THE CHURCH

Threats from within are always more dangerous than persecution from without. The stability of the new church was at stake. Souls were on the line. People were becoming confused and in danger of falling away in discouragement; severe measures were imperative. Keep in mind the sharp condemnation in these verses is aimed at false teachers, not just anyone who slips into legalism. Teachers are held to another standard. Jesus said, "If anyone causes one of these little ones—those who believe in me—to stumble, it would be better for them if a large millstone were hung around their neck and they were thrown into the sea" (Mark 9:42).

A third reason Paul harnesses such strong language hinges on his ultimate goal.

THE APPROVAL OF GOD

"Am I now trying to win the approval of human beings, or of God? Or am I trying to please people? If I were still trying to please people, I would not be a servant of Christ" (Galatians 1:10). Apparently, the false teachers were criticizing Paul, insinuating he was watering down the message in order to make things easy. He just wanted to please people and tell them what they wanted to hear. Ultimately, these troublemakers were accusing Paul of being a people-pleaser.

In fact, they may have noticed he adapted his ministry style according to his audience (1 Corinthians 9:19–23) and hurled that against him. They may have told the Galatians Paul was not telling them the complete story, that back in Jerusalem he preached the necessity of circumcision and adherence to the law (see Galatians 5:11).

Paul makes it abundantly clear what motivates him. Let there be no question—it is the approval of God, not the approval of humans (Galatians 1:10). No one speaks the way Paul does if he or she is just interested in being popular.

How is it with you? What drives you? A desire to please people or a desire to serve and please your Lord and Savior? I had to answer that question when I was faced with being fired from the denomination I grew up in for the sake of the gospel. I am more interested in pleasing God than any person. I wish I could always say that about all the small decisions of my life. But by God's grace, I want that to be the increasing direction and pattern of my life. I pray the same for you.

REFLECTION

What is my understanding of the gospel and when have I defended it?

Why am I tempted to seek the approval of humans rather than of God?

DAY 8

DIVINE
REVELATION

How do you view God? Is he a *rule-maker* or a *grace-giver*? That question is at the heart of the problem the Apostle Paul addresses in his letter to the Galatians. Paul had traveled throughout the region of Galatia establishing churches and preaching the gospel—the liberating good news of salvation and new life in Christ alone. New converts rejoiced in the gospel. They were taught that:

- The *grace* of God was the only source of salvation
- The *cross* of Christ was its sole ground
- *Faith* in the good news was the single means of appropriating the free gift
- *The Holy Spirit* was the actualizing power
- *Full status as sons and daughters of God* had been opened to Gentiles as well as Jews, who were now emancipated from the Old Covenant law and one in Christ. The walls of separation had been brought down.

At one time there was a wall in Berlin, Germany, separating East and West Berlin, communist and free. It stood for twenty-eight years as a boundary marker, a restrictor of freedom, a definer of control, a reminder of bondage. More than 5000 people risked their lives to defy it. Many died trying. But, finally, on November 9, 1989, the Berlin Wall came down. People celebrated and started tearing down the wall long before the bulldozers and wrecking balls arrived. They were overwhelmed with joy as they rejoiced in their newfound liberty.

Just as the Berlin Wall had been a wall of separation, the Old Covenant law, with its many boundaries and regulations, was a wall of separation between Jews and non-Jews. But Christ brought the wall down!

> But now in Christ Jesus you who once were far away have been brought near by the blood of Christ. For he himself is our peace, who has made the two groups one and has destroyed the barrier, the dividing wall of hostility, by setting aside in his flesh the law with its commands and regulations. His purpose was to create in himself one new humanity out of the two, thus making peace. (Ephesians 2:13-15)

The new converts of both Jewish and non–Jewish backgrounds rejoiced in their newfound liberty in the gospel at first. But then some false teachers crept in, following on Paul's footsteps, and began confusing the new believers. The Judaizers, finding their security within the wall, tried to keep it up. Afraid of life outside their closely defined boundaries, they worked to re–erect the walls Paul had destroyed by his grace–alone gospel. They tried to pull the new believers back under a yoke of bondage, insisting the new converts submit to the law in order to be saved, especially emphasizing the prominent Jewish boundary markers.

Commentator G. Walter Hansen explains it this way:

[The Judaizers taught] that it was necessary to belong to the Jewish people in order to receive the full blessing of God. Therefore they required the marks of identity peculiar to the Jewish people: circumcision, sabbath observance and kosher food (see Galatians 2:12–14; 4:10; 5:2–3). . . . The message of the rival teachers struck a responsive chord in the Galatian churches. The Galatian converts may have been feeling a loss of social identity, since their new faith in Christ excluded them from both the pagan temples and the Jewish synagogues. So they sought identification with the Jewish people—God's people—by observing the law. . . Their focus shifted from union with Christ by faith and dependence on the Spirit to identification with the Jewish nation and observance of the law.[5]

Now, as we will see in this chapter, Paul found it necessary not only to defend the gospel, but also *himself*. Back in verse 1 Paul declared he was an authoritative apostle who had not been sent by human appointment, but by Jesus Christ and God the Father. Now in verse 11 Paul begins to defend his message by virtue of its divine origin.

Why did Paul have to defend his divine calling and message? Apparently, the false teachers were telling the Galatians the true teaching came from Jerusalem and was approved by the official apostles there. Paul, they said, had learned it from the leaders in Jerusalem, but was withholding truth from them in order to make things easier for the Gentiles; he was ignoring parts of the message he had learned from the church leaders in Jerusalem.

It was to answer this type of slander and reassert the divine origin of his calling and message that Paul appeals in these next verses:

I want you to know, brothers and sisters, that the gospel I preached is not of human origin. I did not receive it from any man, nor was I taught it; rather, I received it by revelation from Jesus Christ.

For you have heard of my previous way of life in Judaism, how intensely I persecuted the church of God and tried to destroy it. I was advancing in Judaism beyond many of my own age among my people and was extremely zealous for the traditions of my fathers. But when God, who set me apart from my mother's womb and called me by his grace, was pleased to reveal his Son in me so that I might preach him among the Gentiles, my immediate response was not to consult any human being. I did not go up to Jerusalem to see those who were apostles before I was, but I went into Arabia. Later I returned to Damascus.

Then after three years, I went up to Jerusalem to get acquainted with Cephas and stayed with him fifteen days. I saw none of the other apostles—only James, the Lord's brother. I assure you before God that what I am writing you is no lie.

Then I went to Syria and Cilicia. I was personally unknown to the churches of Judea that are in Christ. They only heard the report: "The man who formerly persecuted us is now preaching the faith he once tried to destroy." And they praised God because of me. (Galatians 1:11–24)

On the basis of these verses, we will consider three realities:

THE AUTHORITY OF A DIVINE REVELATION

I want you to know, brothers and sisters, that the gospel I preached is not of human origin. I did not receive it from any

man, nor was I taught it; rather, I received it by revelation
from Jesus Christ. (Galatians 1:11–12)

Paul's gospel was not something he learned from human beings.
He did not go to school to learn it. He did not read it in a book. He
got it directly from Jesus by divine revelation. Paul's burden here is not
to emphasize his independence from the other apostles, but the direct
revelation that he received from Jesus. Independence is not always
a good thing. Responsible Bible students will submit their research,
understanding, and conclusions to others.

But Paul was not just another Bible student like you and me. He
was an apostle. He had come face to face with the risen Lord Jesus who
had commissioned him as an apostle to the Gentiles and given him a
message to preach (Acts 9).

If his message had been given by humans then it could be changed,
adapted, or adjusted by people. But it came from Jesus (via revelation)
and could not be altered. Divine revelation is not the same as an
impression any believer may receive from God. If we are walking in tune
with the Holy Spirit, sometimes we may have promptings or leadings
from him, gentle impressions given with quiet inner conviction.

That is not what Paul is talking about here. "Revelation" is where
God visited *prophets* in the Old Testament era or *apostles* in the New
Testament era and clearly revealed his will and message. When they
wrote down those messages for others under the direction of the Holy
Spirit, they did so through the inspiration of God. God directed their
thoughts and word choices so that what they communicated was his
word.

Above all, you must understand that no prophecy of Scripture
came about by the prophet's own interpretation of things. For
prophecy never had its origin in the human will, but prophets,

though human, spoke from God as they were carried along by
the Holy Spirit. (2 Peter 1:20)

In Galatians 1, Paul makes it clear the gospel he is preaching is not
open for debate. Received by revelation from Jesus, he did not learn it
in Jerusalem.

When did he receive it? Was it when he first saw the risen Lord on
the road to Damascus? Was it during the three days he was blind? Was it
during the three years he spent in the wilderness of Arabia near Damascus?
We do not know. Maybe during that entire time Jesus communicated
with him in various ways to prepare him for his unique calling as an
apostle, preacher to the Gentiles, and author of large portions of the
New Testament Scripture.

It is interesting Paul went to the desert for three years following
his conversion (verse 17). What happened out there? Perhaps, as he
meditated on the Old Testament Scriptures, the grace of God was
revealed to him as never before. Maybe the three years in Arabia was
how Jesus made up for the three years of instruction the other apostles
received. After those three years (which, incidentally, is about how long it
takes to do a Master of Divinity at seminary), Paul had time to recognize
Jesus as the fulfillment of all of the Hebrew Scriptures. He was ready to
preach the Word in light of the cross. He traveled briefly to Jerusalem
(verse 18) to meet Peter and James (the brother of Jesus)—not to learn
from them—but to *get acquainted.* Then he returned to Gentile regions
where he preached the gospel for a number of years before returning to
Jerusalem fourteen years later (Galatians 2:1).

Paul goes to great lengths in these verses to prove his calling and
message were a result of direct revelation from Jesus. The fact that he had
been a vicious persecutor of the church, was then singled out by God
and converted, then alone for three years, then for a number of years
preached the gospel in Gentile areas shows his message was not from

man, but from God. By giving the Galatian readers names of people and places and dates, they could check out the story and confirm if for themselves. When he says, "I assure you by God that what I am writing you is no lie" (verse 20), he is not just saying "please believe me," rather, "Go check it out if you want and verify it."

If you are ever tempted to doubt the authenticity of the New Testament Scriptures, do not forget there was ample opportunity for the recipients of these letters to interview eyewitnesses and fact check the sources. The fact that the documents survived cross–examination bears witness to their authenticity.

REFLECTION

In what ways have I related to God more as rule-maker or grace-giver?

How does the fact that the New Testament was written while eyewitnesses were still alive speak to its reliability?

DAY 9

CALLED
BY GRACE

The first application lesson for us from Galatians 1:11–24 is this message is from God, not Paul. If that is true, we better sit up and listen, take heed, surrender our own opinions, accept what is here, and modify our lives accordingly. My words will not transform your life; it is God's Word that has life–changing power. May we respect God's Word and submit our lives to it.

The main point of this passage is the authority of a divine revelation. I would like you to see two other secondary points of application. Notice secondly:

THE IMPACT OF A PERSONAL TESTIMONY

Paul tells his conversion story in more or less detail in several places. Here he summarizes it briefly. Since he was persecuting the church before his encounter with Jesus, he was well-known among believers, and his conversion came as a big surprise. "They only heard the report: 'The man who formerly persecuted us is now preaching the

faith he once tried to destroy.' And they praised God because of me"
(Galatians 1:23–24).

There is nothing more inspiring and motivating than the testimony
of a transformed life through the power of God. Paul says when they
heard his story "they praised God because of me." Every one of us who
is a Christian has a testimony. You may not have a dramatic testimony
like Paul. Some people can point to a specific time when they became
a Christian, and for others it was a gradual awakening, not dramatic at
all. That does not mean you have no testimony, just a different kind of
testimony.

It is helpful to think through your testimony—even write it out—
so you can clearly share it with others, inspiring them to hear how God
has worked in your life. It might help to organize your testimony in
an outline. Paul tells his story in three parts: 1) My life before I was a
Christian; 2) How I became a Christian; 3) My life after I became a
Christian. That is a logical and applicable outline for any of us to use.

Most people are willing to listen to your story. They may not want
to hear you preach a sermon—they can argue with that—but they
cannot argue with your testimony; it is your story. There is power in a
personal testimony, often with great potential for life–changing impact.
Notice also:

THE POTENTIAL OF A CONVERTED LEGALIST

Please do not ever write anyone off. Who would have thought Paul
would become the foremost apostle of grace? "For you have heard of my
previous way of life in Judaism, how intensely I persecuted the church of
God and tried to destroy it" (Galatians 1:13).

Before his conversion, Paul did not just oppose Christianity, he
persecuted the church. He did not just persecute the church, he *intensely*
persecuted it. He did not just intensely persecute the church, he *tried
to destroy it!* This guy was extreme. "I was advancing in Judaism beyond

many of my own age among my people and was extremely zealous for the traditions of my fathers" (Galatians 1:14).

He did not just hold to Judaism, he *advanced* it. He did not just advance it, he did so *beyond many his own age.* He did not just hold to the Jewish law and traditions, he was *extremely zealous.*

Do you know any legalist like that—extremely zealous for the law, willing to argue, fight, and bully others over their opinions, traditions, and rules? Do you know anyone like that? Do not write them off. Love them. Show grace to them. Pray for them earnestly. If there was hope for Paul to turn around there is hope for any Pharisee, no matter how steeped in legalism. When grace finally got a hold of Paul his life was radically changed.

> But when God, who set me apart from my mother's womb
> and called me by his grace, was pleased to reveal his Son
> in me so that I might preach him among the Gentiles.
> (Galatians 1:15–16)

I love that phrase: *called me by his grace.* Every one of us has been called by his grace—even from our mother's womb and before. None of us are called to be an apostle in the same way as Paul, but we are all called to salvation and called to ministry by God's grace. God's grace initiative comes to each of us. We do not come to God first; he comes to us. His grace was extended to us in Christ "while we were still sinners" (Romans 5:8).

When Paul accepted God's grace initiative, he was sent to preach, and he became one of the greatest advocates for grace who has ever walked on planet earth. But first he needed some time alone, three years in the desert. It took some time for the former legalist to deprogram and reprogram, to fully process the glorious good news of the gospel. A whole package of beliefs he had been so sure of was shattered. A system he had fought to preserve had come crashing down like a house of cards.

Paul took some time to settle into the gospel of grace in Christ Jesus, then he dedicated his life to proclaiming it with steadfast resolve and power. Get this point: the more steeped in legalism a person has been, the more he or she appreciates the gospel once it is fully grasped and accepted.

Paul is a premier example. The Protestant reformer Martin Luther is another foremost example. Some of us can relate because of our own backgrounds in legalism. I can divide my own personal story into three phases:

- Phase one: *Running from Christ*
- Phase two: *Working with Christ*
- Phase three: *Resting in Christ*

After several years of living in the flesh as a rebellious teenager, I realized I could not find peace apart from God, so I turned to him. I experienced peace with God, but I bought into a legalistic system that made salvation partly dependent on me. It was like Jesus handled the down payment, and now I needed to make the monthly installments on my salvation plan. I was no longer running away but instead was working hard to pull off my salvation, along with Christ's help. What a depressing and daunting assignment, trying to accomplish such an impossibility! I had peace *with* God, but not the peace *of* God.

Over time through Scripture, through reading, and through godly believers, I began to mature in my understanding of the gospel until I came to the place where I saw myself as a totally unworthy sinner apart from the perfect, finished work of Christ alone. I finally quit working toward salvation and began resting in it, in Christ alone for security.

If I were to summarize each of those three stages with one word it would be:

- Phase one: *Sinner*. . . living only for myself
- Phase two: *Servant*. . . trying hard to work for God and hopefully earn his favor
- Phase three: *Son*. . . still a sinner, still a servant, but fully forgiven, fully secure in God's family, and now I'm working *from* victory not *toward* victory

Years of living in legalism have downsides—foremost for me would be that I probably discouraged others by trying to place unnecessary yokes of bondage on them. But such a journey offers an upside as well. The Apostle Paul modeled the potential of a converted legalist. No one is as passionately devoted to the gospel of grace as a former legalist. Evaluating my past, I choose to focus on the upside and make the future count for the kingdom, and with all my heart I rejoice that God's grace has set me free. Jesus said, "Now a slave has no permanent place in the family, but a son belongs to it forever. So if the Son sets you free, you will be free indeed" (John 8:35–36).

REFLECTION

How can I use the simple outline mentioned above to write out my testimony?

When have I experienced legalism in my life?

DAY 10

STAND YOUR
GROUND

Most people find major change to be painful. The New Testament has much to say about the stress, controversy, and adaptation—the plain, old–fashioned, painful *change* necessary for people in the first century to transition from the Old Covenant to the New Covenant.

When Jesus came, he ratified a New Covenant of grace available to any person, of any race, who entered through faith into his finished accomplishment. The New Covenant replaced the law–based Old Covenant, which was given at Sinai for the people of Israel. For Jews who became Christians a transition was necessary. This change was not easy, even though it was for the better. Some jumped right into the New Covenant, while others held tenaciously to the Old. Some tried to blend the two, and debates raged over how much of the Old was still binding in the Christian era. Some of those debates are still going on today.

Galatians 1 can be summarized by four simple statements Paul makes:

1) I am an apostle, verse 1

2) I am astonished, verse 6

3) I am preaching a gospel I received by revelation, verse 12

4) I am not lying, verse 20

In the first chapter of Galatians, Paul asserts his gospel was completely *independent* from the church in Jerusalem. It was given to him directly from God. He never even visited Jerusalem until three years after his conversion, and then it was just a brief visit to meet Peter and James.

Now in chapter 2, Paul goes on to show that, although he received his gospel independently from the Jerusalem church, it was an *identical* gospel to theirs, and his message was recognized and affirmed by the church leaders who endorsed his ministry.

> Then after fourteen years, I went up again to Jerusalem, this
> time with Barnabas. I took Titus along also. I went in response
> to a revelation and, meeting privately with those esteemed as
> leaders, I presented to them the gospel that I preach among
> the Gentiles. I wanted to be sure I was not running and had
> not been running my race in vain. (Galatians 2:1–2)

Fourteen years later (probably fourteen years after his conversion), Paul went to Jerusalem and met with some church leaders. Barnabas was a respected Jewish Christian leader, a man who must have been uplifting to be around. In fact, his friends had given him a new name, Barnabas, which means "Son of Encouragement." Barnabas had been one of the early supporters of Paul after his conversion (Acts 9:26–27, 11:22–25), so it was natural for Paul and Barnabas to go together to Jerusalem.

But Titus was a different story. It was Paul's idea to take Titus, a Gentile, along too (2:1). A controversial traveling partner, he would not be allowed in the Jewish synagogues or the temple in Jerusalem because he was uncircumcised. Titus apparently was one of Paul's converts, and he became a fellow minister, missionary, and close companion of Paul's, and one of the New Testament epistles bears his name.

Maybe Paul brought Titus as a trophy of grace and a test case. As a *trophy*, he would provide evidence of the genuine conversion and life transformation happening among the Gentiles. As a *test case*, he would provide opportunity for the attitude of the believers in Jerusalem to be displayed.

When Paul arrived in Jerusalem, he set before the leaders *the gospel that he preached among the Gentiles*. What was that gospel? The simple message of salvation by grace alone, received through faith alone, because of Christ alone—a gospel of free grace apart from works, a gospel which did not require conformity to the law and customs of the Jews, but simply faith in Christ.

Paul arranged a private meeting with the leaders *for fear that he had run the race in vain*. At first glance it looks like Paul was a bit insecure and worried, wondering if he was preaching the right thing—as if he had doubts in his mind from old tapes and needed assurance from the church pillars. Some people read it that way. I do not. Why? Because it comes right after chapter one where Paul has confidently established his gospel came through divine revelation—it was not from men, but from Jesus, and no one could change it, not even an angel from heaven.

I think what Paul is saying here is that he did not want all of his investment for the sake of the gospel to be in vain. He did not want his work and preaching to be undermined by lack of support from Jerusalem. So, he met privately with the leaders to make sure they were on the same page, backing each other up.

> Yet not even Titus, who was with me, was compelled to be circumcised, even though he was a Greek. This matter arose

because some false believers had infiltrated our ranks to spy on
the freedom we have in Christ Jesus and to make us slaves. We
did not give in to them for a moment, so that the truth of the
gospel might be preserved for you. (Galatians 2:3–5)

If Paul brought Titus along as a test case, he ended up being just
that. Paul must have insisted Titus was an equal believer just as he was,
not after he conformed to the law. Remember, circumcision was the
entry sign into the Old Covenant. Circumcision was not the only issue,
but it became a symbol of conformity to the Law of Moses, the entire
Old Covenant package delivered to the Israelites at Mount Sinai.

By bringing Titus along and insisting he remain as he was, Paul
was saying in essence: "Deal with it! We are living in the New Covenant
now, so let us live like it, and move away from mandating Old Covenant
practices!"

I do not think Paul tried to pick a fight. He mainly wanted to speak
with the leaders privately it seems, but legalists can be very aggressive with
their agenda and their insistence on imposing their way on everyone else.
Some false teachers infiltrated the ranks as spies. Maybe that means they
found out about the meetings Paul was having and crashed the party.
The language suggests they snuck in, acting like they were supporters
with a hidden agenda which did not stay hidden for long. Paul says, they
wanted to *spy on the freedom we have in Christ Jesus and to make us slaves.*

Please do not miss the beautiful phrase in the middle of that
sentence: *the freedom we have in Christ Jesus.* That is the theme of
Galatians, and that is the heart of the gospel. When you hide your life
in Christ, and rest secure in him and him alone, you have freedom, a
wonderful freedom found only *in Christ Jesus,* not freedom to go out and
sin and live according to the flesh and be irresponsible, but freedom from
bondage to sin, freedom from guilt, freedom from condemnation—and
more than that—freedom from the law, freedom from an obsession with

lists, regulations, rules, and do's and don'ts, as Paul points out when he says, "If you are led by the Spirit, you are not under the law" (Galatians 5:18). The Spirit leads you, not the law. Likewise, Paul wrote, "Where the Spirit of the Lord is, there is freedom" (2 Corinthians 3:17). There is awesome freedom in letting the Spirit lead and guide through his word and through the inner compass of the conscience.

Paul says the false brothers were spying on the freedom they had in Christ and trying to make them slaves. (I do not want to know what kind of spying they did to find out Titus was uncircumcised!). But please realize it is not the responsibility of believers to spy on other believers.

"Guess who I saw going into the brewery? I guess he drinks beer!"

"Oh, look who is at the theater; I wonder which movie they're going to and what it's rated?"

"Did you know so and so got a tattoo. . . can you believe it?"

When we follow the Lord, allowing him to lead us, we must choose not to worry about how God is leading others to express their freedom. If you have questions about that, read Romans 14. Legalists tend to worry more about other people than themselves, and that always looks ugly.

These guys were trying *to make us slaves,* Paul reports. Slaves to what? Slaves to the law, slaves to a Christ–plus–something gospel, which is why they were demanding Titus be circumcised. Freedom is a precious thing. No one should have to go back into slavery after having tasted freedom: "We did not give in to them for a moment, so that the truth of the gospel might be preserved for you" (Galatians 2:5).

Paul was determined whenever *the truth of the gospel* was at stake he would stand up for it. He says *we did not give in to them for a moment.* I had to smile while writing this because in the background I am listening to the words in Tom Petty's song, "I Won't Back Down":

Well, I won't back down
No, I won't back down

You can stand me up at the gates of hell
But I won't back down

That sounds like Paul! He was going to stand his ground and not back down. Does that mean he was a bullheaded and argumentative guy who had to have his own way on everything? No, not at all. Paul took a totally different approach with *weak* believers (See 1 Corinthians 8 and Romans 14) than he did with *false* believers. These were *false believers* (verse 4). Paul also took a totally different approach when dealing with opposing opinions versus deviant gospels. Whenever someone started making a salvation issue out of anything and adding it to the gospel of grace, Paul immediately identified it as heresy and confronted it aggressively.

Let me show you how differently Paul could relate to the same issue depending on whether it was an issue of relating to *weak* or *false* believers, and depending on whether it was an issue of different *opinions* or different *gospels*. Look at the three main Jewish boundary marker issues: circumcision, food rules, and holy days.

- **Circumcision** – Paul (at a later time, after the Jerusalem Council, where it was decided circumcision was not a salvation issue) had another missionary, Timothy, get circumcised (Acts 16:3). Why? Timothy was half Jew. Apparently, he had great potential to reach Jews with the gospel, but he would need to enter their synagogues and be accepted by them before he could lead them to Christ. So, Paul had Timothy circumcised "because of the Jews" (Acts 16:3). It was not a salvation issue here, it was a concession to weakness and for strategic ministry purposes. But back in Jerusalem, earlier with Titus, who was a full–blooded Gentile, with no potential or calling to a Jewish evangelistic mission, and with the Judaizers trying to make a salvation issue out of it, Paul *did not give in for one minute.*

- **Food Rules** – In 1 Corinthians 8 and 10, Paul encourages believers to place certain limits on their liberty if a weak believer may be confused or discouraged by the exercise of freedom in some area, such as eating food offered to idols. This was not a salvation issue and some people had opposing opinions. Paul asked believers to be respectful of different views. But his tone about food laws is radically different in 1 Timothy 4:1–5. Apparently, false teachers were mandating certain foods were not to be eaten, making this a salvation issue. Paul reacts forcefully and calls that a "doctrine of demons."

- **Holy Days** – By holy days I mean the Jewish holy days listed in Leviticus 23, which included the weekly Sabbath, monthly new moons, and annual festivals. In Colossians 2:16–17 and Romans 14:5–6, Paul says "do not judge" people who consider certain days holy. Those verses were written regarding the weak and those who had different opinions but were not making a salvation issue out of it. But notice the difference in tone on the same subject in Galatians 4:10–11. There he does not say "don't judge. . . let each of you be fully convinced in your own mind. . ." No! He says, "I fear for you. . . seems like I have wasted my efforts!" Why? Because the Judaizers had made the observance of Jewish holy days a salvation issue.

Back to the Scripture: "We did not give in to them for a moment, so that the truth of the gospel might be preserved for you" (Galatians 2:5). Does it make sense to you why Paul takes the approach he does here? The issue was *the truth of the gospel*. Whenever the truth of the gospel is at stake because of false teachers or legalistic beliefs it must be uncompromisingly defended.

REFLECTION

What does the phrase "the freedom we have in Christ Jesus" mean to me?

When have I had to stand my ground to maintain that freedom?

DAY 11

A DIFFICULT
TRANSITION

Why was it so hard for many of the Jewish Christians to make the transition from the Old Covenant to the New Covenant? The answer is complex because people are complex. Many factors combined to make change difficult: cultural, social, behavioral, psychological, theological, and pride issues were all wrapped up together. Think about each one of these and how they impact change (then and now).

ISSUES IMPACTING CHANGE

1. Cultural Issues

People find security in the familiar, in the rules, boundaries, and traditions with which they have grown up. We are creatures of habit. That makes change hard.

2. Social Issues

If you have family or friends or work associates or schoolmates who are putting pressure on you to conform to the old way, it is hard to resist.

If you do not conform, it usually affects those relationships negatively, and that is uncomfortable.

3. Behavioral Issues

Humans tend naturally to resist change and hang on to the familiar, some more than others, since we all have different personality styles. Behavioral scientists have noted that within the general population there is a bell curve:

- 2.5 percent are *Innovators* – they like to take risks and are able to change quickly
- 14 percent are *Early Adopters* – they are pioneer types and opinion leaders
- 34 percent are *Early Majority* – they are willing to change after the opinion leaders do
- 34 percent are *Late Majority* – they are hesitant, skeptical, and cautious, accepting change only after the early majority does
- 16 percent are *Laggards* – they are traditional, resistant, suspicious, and focused on the past[6]

Behaviorally speaking, some people are always going to be more resistant than others to change, at least at first.

4. Psychological Issues

Psychologists study the way the mind works, and they often disagree. But most theorists are in consensus concerning something called "cognitive consistency." "Cognitive consistency is a technical term employed to describe the tendency within almost all of us to keep our attitudes, behaviors, and perceptions consistent."[7] If we feel our beliefs are being significantly challenged or changed, it throws us out of balance into an inconsistent state of mind called "cognitive dissonance."

The theory of cognitive consistency "holds that such a change produces psychological tension which we seek to reduce by either distorting the new message or by changing some other part of the system. This response is motivated by our strong desire to regain a state of consistency."[8]

Author and professor Duane Liftin writes:

Our desire for a balanced system also explains the phenomenon of 'selective perception.' It is commonly recognized that people tend to avoid messages which contradict their views. . . the reason for this is that contrary messages tend to arouse the tension which stems from inconsistency. Since the easiest way to deal with this tension is to prevent it from arising in the first place, people commonly listen only to those with who they already agree. In this way a comfortable balance can be maintained. There are few postulates of modern psychology which are as widely accepted and as solidly based as this assertion: people desire mental consistency and strive to maintain it, often at the expense of the truth.[9]

You see this not only in theological but also political debates: "Don't confuse me with the facts, I know what I want to believe," seems to be a common attitude. Some definite psychological issues make a radical transition—like moving from the Old Covenant to the New Covenant—very difficult.

5.   Theological Issues

When a group of people are convinced they are the people of God and believe they can back it up with Scripture, they tend to develop an "us–versus–them" mentality. They are the chosen ones, the remnant, the apple of God's eye, the ones on the path of light, the right ship that is going through the storm to the end. Everyone else is on the outside. Security comes from an easily recognizable set of boundaries—a detailed package of doable stuff that defines who is on the inside and who is on the outside. In this type of system, it becomes impossible to imagine anyone being saved if they do not become a part of the chosen few.

6.   Pride Issues

All of us have a natural, sinful, internal pull toward selfishness and pride. Legalism, like all false religion, appeals to the flesh because it is a human–centered approach, motivated by human achievement. Since much of the Jewish system had degenerated into legalism, there were pride issues inhibiting the grace awakening.

Why was it so daunting for many of the Jewish Christians to make the transition from the Old Covenant to the New Covenant? It's a complex answer, which includes cultural, social, behavioral, psychological, theological, and pride issues all wrapped up together. That was true for the Jewish Christians in first century Jerusalem, and it is true for some today as well.

Many resisted the transition to the New Covenant and wanted to drag new believers back under the law. But Paul held firm: "We did not give in to them for a moment, so that the truth of the gospel might be preserved for you" (Galatians 2:5).

Now notice the consequences of Paul's summit with the church leaders. The leaders affirmed three things: Paul's message, his strategy, and his calling.

PAUL'S MESSAGE

"As for those who were held in high esteem—whatever they were makes no difference to me; God does not show favoritism—they added nothing to my message" (Galatians 2:6). They added nothing to the message. This is an important point. They were preaching the same message. They did not see a need to add a thing (contrary to what the false teachers were telling the churches in Galatia).

PAUL'S STRATEGY

"On the contrary, they recognized that I had been entrusted with the task of preaching the gospel to the uncircumcised, just as Peter had been to the circumcised" (Galatians 2:7). Peter ministered in Judea, and his main target group was Jews. Paul ministered throughout the Roman Empire, and his primary target was Gentiles. Sometimes Christians get the idea that every church or ministry should have the exact same look, feel, style, focus, and target group. Not so. We all must hold to the exact same gospel, but beyond that God can use us more powerfully to reach as many as possible if various churches and ministries diversify and target different peoples.

PAUL'S CALLING

> For God, who was at work in Peter as an apostle to the circumcised, was also at work in me as an apostle to the Gentiles. James, Cephas and John, those esteemed as pillars, gave me and Barnabas the right hand of fellowship when they recognized the grace given to me. They agreed that we should go to the Gentiles, and they to the circumcised. All they asked was that we should continue to remember the poor, the very thing I had been eager to do all along. (Galatians 2:8–10)

This was quite a group of leaders gathered in one place. At least twenty-one out of the twenty-seven New Testament epistles were written by these men. It must have been extremely affirming for Paul, after he missed out on the official launch of the church and dedicated a stretch of his life to stamping out the church, to now have this group of leaders who had walked with Jesus *recognize* his calling.

A divine calling is not bestowed by men—only recognized. They recognized his calling and extended him the *right hand of fellowship*. They officially endorsed his God–ordained ministry. They said, "God bless you, keep up the good work. . . and don't forget the poor." Since there was a high concentration of poverty in Jerusalem, it appears this was a way of saying: "Go reach the Gentiles, but maintain a link with the church in Jerusalem by raising some support for the needy here." Paul responded that was *the very thing* he was *eager to do*. In fact, it was one of the reasons he had come in the first place, and throughout the letters he would later write it was a reoccurring theme as he gathered offerings for the poor.

In this passage, Paul provides an example of appropriate respect toward those who are in leadership in the church. Those in authority should be submitted to and honored—unless they are *not in line with the truth of the gospel*, in which case a higher authority kicks in. (We will see an example of that in the next chapter).

If anyone understood this issue it was Protestant Reformer Martin Luther during his confrontations with the established Roman Catholic Church of his day. Even at great risk to his life, Luther boldly stood up for the gospel. Listen to his words:

> If the Pope will grant unto us that God alone by His mere grace through Christ does justify sinners, we will not only carry him in our hands, but will also kiss his feet. But since we cannot obtain this, we in God will give no place, no, not one hair's breadth, to all the angels in heaven, not to Peter, not to Paul, not to a hundred emperors, nor a thousand popes, nor to the whole world. Let this be then the conclusion: that we will suffer our goods to be taken away, our name, our life, and all that we have; but the gospel, our faith, Jesus Christ, we will never suffer to be wrested from us.[10]

To that, all I can add is "amen." Whenever legalists try to add to the gospel or impose their way on others, we should kindly yet firmly respond like Paul and not give in to them. Many of us have struggled to one degree or another with a painful transition from legalism to grace. Once we understand and embrace the gospel, we do well to stand for it, defend it, and cherish the precious freedom we have in Christ Jesus.

REFLECTION

Do I find change easy or difficult? Where do I fall on the bell curve between "innovative leader" and "laggard"?

Where have I seen examples of where cultural, social, behavioral, psychological, theological, or pride issues have made transition difficult?

DAY 12

CONFRONTING
HYPOCRISY

There is a switch inside your mind called "imagination." I want to ask you to turn it on. Okay? Imagine with me.

The church had been growing rapidly. It started with just a handful in a living room. As people began to understand the good news of the gospel of grace in Christ Jesus their lives were radically changed. They began to tell their friends and neighbors about their newfound treasure. More and more people came and soon the living room was packed, standing room only. New people invited the pastor to come hold meetings in their homes. Small group leaders were trained, and before long there were multiple locations around the city where believers met to study the Bible, pray, and encourage each other in the faith. Small meeting rooms and then larger public auditoriums were rented for weekly services where all the small groups would gather for worship and teaching. The numbers mushroomed from dozens to hundreds, and then many hundreds. Sometimes it was necessary to hold services outdoors so everyone could gather together.

There was incredible momentum and energy in the church. People could hardly wait to get together. Various social classes, races, and ages worshipped side by side in full acceptance of each other. The rich helped the poor. No one went hungry or homeless or lacked for any necessities. Conflicts were rare and resolved quickly because everyone was committed to unity in the Spirit.

Someone had an idea. "Our church has grown so fast in the few years since it was planted. We're coming up on an anniversary date. Why don't we have a grand celebration of what God has done in our midst?" Everyone loved the idea and preparations were made. The plan was to have an entire week of festivities with guest speakers and musicians in the evening and an all–day blowout on the final day with worship, teaching, fellowship, food, and fun. They sent invitations, outlined services, and planned meals.

Pastor Paul surprised and thrilled everyone when he announced Pastor Simon Peter from Jerusalem was traveling to Antioch for the celebration. He would stay the whole week and present a number of messages. Of course, everyone was anxious for Peter to arrive; after all, he had spent over three years hanging out in person with Jesus. So many offers of hospitality came into the church office that Associate Pastor Barnabas made out a schedule placing Peter at different homes each night during his stay, enabling more families to entertain him and ask him questions over a meal. more families would be able to entertain him and ask him questions over a meal.

The long–anticipated day arrives and with it, Peter. He is thrilled to see the progress of the church in Antioch. People hang on his every word as he salts his sermons with behind–the–scenes stories about Jesus. He enjoys the warm hospitality shown him. One morning Peter wakes up to the smell of bacon cooking, and it smells good, but for just a moment an old recording starts to play in his mind. He feels a twinge of guilt for staying with a non-Jewish family. No doubt they will serve him bacon, maybe some sausage. Jews do not eat pork. Jews do not eat with Gentiles.

But just as soon as that old tape starts, another tape turns on in Peter's mind, drowning out the old one. "Come on, Peter. You have moved past those old hang-ups. You are living in the New Covenant. The Old Covenant has passed away. There is no more separation; these people are your brothers and sisters. We are all one in Christ, so do not worry what they feed you, because it does not matter anymore." A smile comes across Peter's face as he lies in bed a few more moments reflecting. He remembers how hard it was for him to change his thinking initially. What a paradigm shift. He chuckles out loud as he recalls the funny rooftop vision God gave him. He can still see the vision in living color in his memory: a sheet filled with all kinds of animals was lowered and God said, "Select something for lunch and cook it." Peter recoiled and said, "No way. . . I've never eaten anything unclean." The vision came three times with the same message, followed immediately by a knock on the door downstairs. Three men stood at the door asking Peter to come and teach the gospel to their Gentile master, Cornelius. Peter went and preached and ate with Cornelius and his family. It felt strange at first, but it was such a joy to see that whole household accept the good news. The walls of separation started to crumble.

"I'm so glad for the freedom of the New Covenant," Peter thinks to himself. "It doesn't matter if they are not Jews, are not circumcised, serve bacon, do not prepare food according to Jewish customs—or even if the food has been previously offered to idols before sold in the market. I'm free of all that. But," Peter laughs out loud and whispers to himself, "God really had to get creative to get my attention." Just then someone knocks on the bedroom door and informs Peter that breakfast is ready. He pulls on fresh clothes and enjoys some rich fellowship over toast, eggs, and bacon.

The next day a delegation of elders from Jerusalem arrives just in time for the weekend celebrations. They are a stuffy lot, Jewish Christians, with the emphasis on *Jewish*. It quickly becomes apparent they are more interested in spying to see if the new converts are being taught all the Jewish laws, rather than joining in the celebration. Their leader, Ben, comes unglued when he sees an invitation that says the lunch after church will be at a Gentile family's farm on the outskirts of the city. He pulls Peter aside and chides him for letting this go on. "You're not going to attend that, are you, Peter?" Ben inquires.

"Why, sure I'm going," Peter replies. "Everyone will be there. That dinner is a big part of the festivities."

Ben gives a grunt of disgust. "Can't you see, Peter, that these compromises are ruining our faith? We're losing the uniqueness of our heritage. They'll probably have a pig roasting, with an apple in its mouth!"

"What difference does it make?" Peter retorts. "You don't have to eat any pork roast if you still have scruples about that or if you have not developed a taste for it. That is understandable. There will be other food."

"You're missing the point, Peter," huffs Ben. "You are endorsing what is going on by even showing up there. Why don't you just skip the lunch and show up for the evening meeting. You do not want to undercut your influence in Jerusalem, do you, Peter? We have to let Gentiles in the church, but we do not have to eat with them. If you do, you might as well write off any chance of continued leadership in Jerusalem. This has become a huge issue ever since you opened the doors to the Gentiles, and now people are getting fed up with the direction of things. This church in Antioch is just throwing everything out. Paul is a problem. He's not balanced. He is overreacting to his past fanaticism. He is going too far, throwing the baby out with the bath water. He acts like he has a chip on his shoulder and is out to undermine Judaism. Anyone can see it. A lot of people are talking about it. Okay, so God wants us to let some Gentiles into the church, but they must be circumcised and obey all the law. It is the Word of God we're talking about here, Peter!"

A small crowd of leaders has gathered at this point. Barnabas is listening in and gives his opinion. "I can see what you're saying, Ben. I struggle sometimes with how to relate to Moses these days, but please understand we don't want to offend our brothers and sisters who are not Jews. Their feelings will be hurt if we don't go to the lunch."

"Too bad," Ben replies briskly. "Sometimes feelings must be hurt in order to stand for truth and make a point."

The day of celebration arrives. After the morning worship service, a group of believers gathers for lunch. But the gathering is much smaller than anticipated. Peter and Barnabas and most of the Jewish Christians are notably absent. Word gets out that Peter has decided not to eat with Gentiles and has influenced others as well. There is confusion, disappointment, discouragement, and frustration. Little groups gather. The discussion is animated. "Why? What's going on?"

Pastor Paul is in deep thought during the meal. He wanders around and listens in on several conversations. Finally, he dismisses himself saying he must make final preparations for his evening message. As the senior leader of the church in Antioch it is appropriate that he speak at the last meeting. He has planned to review God's leading in the congregation and cast vision for the future. He takes a late–afternoon walk hoping to sort his thoughts out. He is disturbed in his spirit. "Will there end up being two churches, one for the Jews and one for the Gentiles?" he wonders. "Or will the Gentiles have to become Jews to avoid being treated as second–class citizens in the church? Should I ignore this and just hope it will go away, or should I confront it? Peter was in the wrong today. Should I talk to him one-on-one? After all, Jesus taught to go privately to someone who has offended you. But," he reminds himself, "this was a public issue. Everyone is talking about it. When I get up to speak tonight there will be an elephant in the room that will get in the way if I don't address it."

Paul wrinkles his brow as he walks, deep in thought. "Is it just an issue of personal opinion we're dealing with here?" he wonders. "No," he answers himself, "this is an affront on the gospel. Either the gospel brings down barriers, or it does not. Either we are justified apart from the law, or we are not. Either we are all equal in Christ, or we are not. The gospel is at stake," Paul concludes. "I *must* address this issue head on."

At the evening meeting the auditorium is packed. The honored leaders sit at the front. Paul waits for his turn through a few songs, a testimony, an offering, and a prayer. Paul senses the congregation is not quite as joyful as they were during the morning service when Peter spoke. A bit of strain and tension can be felt in the air. Pastor Paul takes his place behind the podium. He scans the audience for a moment and then begins to speak—slowly, haltingly, choosing each word carefully. With love and tears in his voice he shares his heart. He talks about his love for Christ and the gospel. He emphasizes the inclusive nature of the gospel.

Then he startles the audience by saying, "But the precious unity that we have in Christ is being threatened. In fact, the gospel is being subtly attacked by those who are not walking consistently with the truth of the gospel." Lest anyone miss the point, the pastor gets specific. "Some of you didn't show up at the meal today for the wrong reasons. Please, friends, let us realize the gospel is Christ–plus–nothing! We are not justified by the law." For the next hour or so, Paul preaches the good news of salvation by grace alone, received by faith, apart from any works. He passionately appeals for the whole community of faith to live free from hypocrisy, modeling for each other the same kind of love and acceptance Jesus demonstrated.

That night Peter cannot sleep. He tosses and turns. He realizes his influence really counts, that people are watching. They can be discouraged or even turned off to Christianity if they see hypocrisy, and rightfully, Peter prays to the Lord and humbly repents.

A few months later the Jerusalem Council gathers to decide whether or not the Gentiles must be circumcised and obey all the Jewish laws (see Acts 15). In the middle of the meeting Peter jumps to his feet and says: "Brothers, you all know that God chose me from among you long ago to preach the Good News to the Gentiles so that they also could believe. God, who knows men's hearts, confirmed the fact that he accepts Gentiles by giving them the Holy Spirit, just as he gave him to us. He made no distinction between them and us, for he cleansed their lives through faith, just as he did ours.

"And now are you going to correct God by burdening the Gentiles with a yoke that neither we nor our fathers were able to bear? Don't you believe that all are saved the same way, by the free gift of the Lord Jesus?"

After Peter's speech, the discussion was over. The council of Christian leaders agreed together that the new Gentile converts were *not* subject to the law, and for the rest of his life Peter stayed determined to keep the barriers down.

Now, I do not know if the story happened just like that or not. But it might have been close, and if you allowed yourself to get into the feelings of that imaginary story at all, then you'll better understand the situation that presents itself in Galatians 2:11–16.

REFLECTION

When have I been led to confront hypocrisy or been confronted myself? When have I been afraid to confront?

Have I struggled with old tapes playing in my head that try to rob me of freedom in Christ?

DAY 13

IN LINE WITH THE TRUTH OF THE GOSPEL

Although I added a few imaginary details here and there in the last chapter, the story is written like this: "When Cephas came to Antioch, I opposed him to his face, because he stood condemned" (Galatians 2:11).

The general pattern of Christian living is not to go around opposing people. In fact, the Bible says to make every effort to preserve the unity of the Spirit; to live in peace with each other if at all possible; to accept each other; to avoid judging; and to allow liberty on nonessential issues. But whenever the truth of the gospel is at stake it is a time to oppose.

Notice that Paul opposed Peter *to his face*; he did not talk about him behind his back. It is always easier to gossip behind someone's back than speak right to them. Paul did not do that. He opposed him to his face *because Peter was clearly in the wrong*. Why was he in the wrong? The next verse tells us:

For before certain men came from James, he used to eat
with the Gentiles. But when they arrived, he began to draw
back and separate himself from the Gentiles because he was
afraid of those who belonged to the circumcision group.
(Galatians 2:12)

This delegation from Jerusalem claimed they were *from James*.
Since James was the respected leader of the church in Jerusalem,
they used his name to try to establish some authority. These men are
called *the circumcision group* which indicates they were Judaizers—
Jewish Christians who were teaching a Christ–plus–something gospel.
They accepted the reality of Christ as the Messiah, but they insisted
circumcision and obedience to the Old Covenant law was also necessary
for salvation.

Here is how Peter was *clearly in the wrong*. The text says, *He used
to eat with the Gentiles* before the legalists arrived. Strict Jews avoided
any social interaction with Gentiles, considering them unclean, and it
was especially offensive to eat with them, since eating involved close
fellowship, and because Jews observed strict food taboos. Of course, Peter
knew those taboos were no longer in effect under the New Covenant for
he had heard Jesus prepare the way for this understanding when he said:

"Are you so dull?" he asked. "Don't you see that nothing that
enters a person from the outside can defile him? For it doesn't
go into their heart but into their stomach, and then out of
the body." (In saying this, Jesus declared all foods clean).
(Mark 7:18–19)

Peter had obtained a firsthand revelation concerning this matter
when he received a vision of unclean animals and God said: "Do not call
anything impure that God has made clean" (Acts 10:15).

Peter and Paul both agreed on this issue. Paul wrote:

I am convinced, being fully persuaded in the Lord Jesus, that
nothing is unclean in itself. But if anyone regards something as
unclean, then for that person it is unclean. . . Do not destroy
the work of God for the sake of food. All food is clean, but it
is wrong for a person to eat anything that causes someone else
to stumble. (Romans 14:14, 20)

Peter understood the Old Covenant regulations were no longer
binding under the New Covenant. It was fine for people to avoid a
specific food because of personal taste or for dietary reasons but not as a
religious requirement. Peter knew it and believed it; he even lived it out,
eating with the Gentiles. The problem was he changed his behavior when
the Christ–plus–something gang came to town. Verse 12 says he *began
to draw back and separate.* Whenever someone begins to "draw back and
separate" from other believers this indicates a problem. Scripture exhorts
us to press together. Jesus prayed for complete unity in the church—
for a community of oneness (John 17). The enemy is always seeking
to disrupt unity, and he will use whatever tactics he can: unresolved
conflict resulting in bitterness, hurt feelings that are nursed, suspicion
and criticism of leadership—you name it. If Satan can destroy unity in
the church, he throws a party. In this case he used false doctrine and fear
of reputation to spoil community. Drawing back and separating is not
the fruit of the gospel.

The text says Peter was *afraid* of the circumcision group. I think it
was a prideful fear of reputation, not a genuine fear. Remember Peter
was one of the bravest of all the disciples. He is the one who drew a
sword to defend Jesus in the Garden of Gethsemane, and yet that same
night he struggled with selfish pride and worried about his reputation,
denying he knew Jesus to a servant girl.

Now notice the result of Peter's influence: "The other Jews joined him in his hypocrisy, so that by their hypocrisy even Barnabas was led astray" (Galatians 2:13). Even Barnabas, who was known for his encouraging, reconciling spirit, was led astray by Peter's hypocrisy. If you are a follower of Jesus, never underestimate the power of your influence. People are looking at you, and some people may be led to Christ or turned away from him by what they see. We are the only Bible some people will read. Nothing turns people off quicker than hypocrisy, when someone talks one way and lives another, and that applies to every Christ follower. Of course, the more influence we have the more responsibility we have to live consistently with what we believe. We are each one accountable to God.

Hypocrisy is not limiting your personal freedom for the sake of a weak Christian. That is a commendable thing. In fact, it is encouraged in Scripture. In this case hypocrisy is kowtowing to legalists. Have you ever been tempted to act contrary to the way you really believe in order to preserve your reputation with legalists? Be careful that you do not quietly endorse their legalism and subtly undermine the gospel by such behavior.

Because of his leadership position, Peter led others astray by his example. So, Paul felt compelled to confront him:

> When I saw that they were not acting in line with the truth
> of the gospel, I said to Cephas in front of them all, "You are
> a Jew, yet you live like a Gentile and not like a Jew. How is
> it, then, that you force Gentiles to follow Jewish customs?"
> (Galatians 2:14)

Peter was not *acting in line with the truth of the gospel.* How would he have acted if he was in line with the truth of the gospel, living consistently? He would have stood openly for what he believed; lived in freedom and let others live in freedom; moved past Old Covenant restrictions; and resisted erecting unbiblical walls of separation and bondage.

Paul confronted Peter *in front of them all*, and there is a place for public confrontation, though most confrontation should be private. Jesus taught about the steps for conflict resolution by saying, "If your brother sins against you, go and show him his fault, just between the two of you. If he listens to you, you have won your brother over (Matthew 18:15). But sometimes public confrontation is necessary, especially when an issue has already become public and the gospel or the preservation of the community is at stake.

In essence, Paul said, "Come on, Peter. You do not live by the Old Covenant requirements. You do not live like a Jew. And now you are going to lend your influence to these Judaizers who are pushing circumcision? If you do that, you are a hypocrite. There is not a problem with people following customs or traditions. The problem is when they *force* those customs or traditions on others. You are lending influence to false teachers who want to force a way of life you yourself do not observe!"

I am sure it was not easy for Paul to stand up to Peter publicly. I am sure he did it in love and humility. He was not trying to be argumentative or push his own agenda; he did it for one reason: for the sake of the gospel. Paul was passionately committed to preserving the truth of the gospel. This is clear in the next verses where he launches into the theological section of the book—the heart of the message to the Galatians.

We will look briefly at the next two verses and then come back to these same verses in the next chapter:

"We who are Jews by birth and not sinful Gentiles know that a person is not justified by the works of the law, but by faith in Jesus Christ. So we, too, have put our faith in Christ Jesus that we may be justified by faith in Christ and not by the works of the law, because by the works of the law no one will be justified." (Galatians 2:15–16)

Paul says to Peter, "You and I were born and raised with the law. We are Jews. We are not like the Gentiles who never knew the law. But no matter how hard we tried to keep the law perfectly, we still fell short. We could not be made right before God by our works, so we have put our faith in Christ Jesus, who has justified us, made us right with God by faith alone, not by observing the law. So," Paul is saying, "Let us live like it. Let us avoid hypocrisy by living out the truth of the gospel. Let us never give anyone the impression they can add to Christ's perfect work in order to get saved or stay saved. That is impossible. Jesus paid it all, one hundred percent."

Imagine a man before a judge who has been given the choice of paying $1,000 or serving ninety days in jail. The man has no money but has an invalid wife and five hungry children at home who are depending on him and him alone. He tells such a heartrending story the courtroom spectators are moved with pity and take up a collection to help pay the man's fine. Although it is unlike him, even the judge chips in. Together they raise $999.95. But even though they are only five cents short, the judge declares the entire $1,000 must be paid and orders the bailiff to take the man to jail.

The condemned man walks dejectedly out of the courtroom, thrusting his hands deep into his pockets. . . where he finds, to his surprise, a nickel. Elated, he rushes back into the courtroom and slaps it on the bar before the judge, declaring, "I'm free, I'm free!" In his mind, what saved him? The $999.95 or the five cents? If we did anything to merit our salvation, we would be forever boasting about it in heaven, and the fact is, we can do nothing because Jesus paid it all.[11]

Our debt of sin is far greater than $1,000. The only way to pay our debt is to die, for the wages of sin is death (Romans 6:23). But as the

Apostle John reminds us, "God so loved the world that he gave his one and only Son, that whoever believes in him shall not perish but have eternal life" (John 3:16).

REFLECTION

When have I been tempted to act contrary to the way I really believe in order to preserve my reputation or fit in?

What does the phrase "not in line with the truth of the gospel" mean to me?

DAY 14

JUSTIFIED BY FAITH

D id you ever have to change schools when you were a kid? I had to do that six or seven times. Can you remember what it felt like to go to a strange new school the first day? Maybe you had a fitful night's sleep the night before—worrying, wondering, and fretting. You woke up on the first day of school with a pit in your stomach. It was hard to eat breakfast. You were not hungry. What should you wear? Picking the right clothing combination is a huge decision with potentially serious consequences. The mirror must be consulted numerous times to make sure your hair is making the correct statement.

And then there is the decision to make regarding the most strategic way to make your first entrance into the classroom. Should you get there early and risk sitting in the wrong place or appearing too studious? Should you come in a little late and sit wherever there is an open seat? Probably not. If you did that everyone would probably stare at you, and you might end up on the front row. That would be terrible.

Why is it a bit scary to go to a new school? Because every human being wants to be accepted, and we feel insecure until we know we are accepted. It is a basic principle, and it is the way we are designed. We long for acceptance and are unfulfilled without it. Within all of us there is a deep desire for acceptance, not only with other people, but especially with God. Our life feels incomplete if we do not sense we are accepted by God. This is a universal reality for all people. Most people recognize there is a God. They may use a variety of words to describe him, and some even have trouble admitting it, but most people believe God exists. God has made himself known—even to those who have never read the Bible, gone to church, or heard a sermon.

> For since the creation of the world God's invisible qualities—his eternal power and divine nature—have been clearly seen, being understood from what has been made, so that people are without excuse. (Romans 1:20)

Furthermore, most people believe God not only exists, but that he is a righteous judge who will demand an account someday. Most people, regardless of what they have been taught or how they live, have a basic sense of right and wrong. No matter how much they do wrong, they believe in their heart they should do right, and that is because God created us each with a conscience:

> Indeed, when Gentiles, who do not have the law, do by nature things required by the law, they are a law for themselves, even though they do not have the law. They show that the requirements of the law are written on their hearts, their consciences also bearing witness, and their thoughts sometimes accusing them and at other times even defending them. (Romans 2:14–15)

Because humans naturally seek acceptance with God, numerous religious systems have been devised. With the exception of one, all the world's religious systems teach that to find acceptance with God you must do or not do certain things. In the end God will judge you, and if your good deeds outweigh your bad deeds, you will be granted a place in the eternal realm.

The problem with all those religious systems is they are fatally flawed. God is a holy and righteous judge, so holy and so righteous that his standard is perfection. He cannot accept sin, any sin, even one sin. Sin would defile and spoil his perfect universe; it cannot be tolerated. Any system that relies on stacking up good deeds to weigh against bad deeds is a dead-end street, because no one can be good enough to satisfy the expectations of God's righteousness, and everyone is already too defiled by sin and selfishness to ever qualify for heaven.

Christianity, rightly understood, stands alone with the answer to the human dilemma. The answer is a person, and his name is Jesus. How can you find acceptance with God? There is only one way—through God's loving provision in his son Jesus, the divine substitute, the holy one who took our place, lived a perfect life, died every sinner's death, and rose from the grave triumphant over sin, death, and the devil. God's Word declares that acceptance with God, justification, can only be attained by faith in Jesus Christ. That is the *truth of the gospel.*

In the previous chapter we examined the story found in Galatians 2:11 and onward. Paul tells how he found it necessary to confront Peter because of his hypocrisy. It is not enough to hear and understand and believe and accept the gospel, it must also be applied. Peter had not applied the gospel consistently. When he first visited the church in Antioch, he lived like a New Covenant Christian. He did not worry about the Old Covenant prohibitions and ate with the Gentiles. But when some Christ–plus–something Judaizers came to town Peter withdrew from eating with the Gentiles for fear he would spoil his reputation back in Jerusalem. So Paul confronted him because he was *not acting in line with the truth of the gospel.* Peter's hypocrisy was damaging because it was subtly undermining the good news of salvation by grace through faith.

What is the "truth of the gospel" Paul refers to? Listen to commentator John Stott's clear summary:

> What, then, is the truth of the gospel? Every reader of the Epistle to the Galatians should know the answer to this question. It is the good news that we sinners, guilty and under the judgment of God, may be pardoned and accepted by His sheer grace, His free and unmerited favor, on the ground of His Son's death and not for any works or merits of our own. More briefly, the truth of the gospel is the doctrine of justification (which means acceptance before God) by grace alone through faith alone. . . [12]

That is what Paul is saying as he continues:

> "We who are Jews by birth and not sinful Gentiles know that a person is not justified by the works of the law, but by faith in Jesus Christ. So we, too, have put our faith in Christ Jesus that we may be justified by faith in Christ and not by the works of the law, because by the works of the law no one will be justified." (Galatians 2:15–16)

In verse 16 we are introduced for the first time in Galatians to a new word—*justified.* What does it mean? "Justification" is a legal term that comes out of the courtroom setting. In a typical court of law, if a person is put on trial for a crime and found guilty, the result is condemnation; if they are found innocent the result is justification (and acquittal). Used theologically, justification means to be accepted by God, to be declared right before God. The good news of the gospel is that we have been justified freely by God's grace through faith in Christ. That means when we accept God's provision in Christ we are accepted by God. We do not have to worry, or work, or be insecure hoping someday we will be accepted by God, for when we lay hold of the free gift of grace, we are in the family. We are justified.

REFLECTION

When did I first realize I could be accepted by God in spite of my past, present, or future accomplishments or failures? Do I struggle believing it?

What does it mean to me to be accepted and pardoned by his "sheer grace" independent of any works or merit on my own?

DAY 15

PEACE
WITH GOD

Although justification is a courtroom term, its biblical meaning goes beyond the courtroom meaning. In the courtroom setting, those who are rightly accused of wrong are condemned. Those who are falsely accused of wrong are justified. But in the gospel, there is a twist. All of us are sinners. We are all rightly accused. We are guilty. But by faith in God's grace provision we are nevertheless justified and acquitted in spite of what we deserve. And we are not just pardoned, we are treated as though we had never sinned and are, in fact, perfectly righteous—because in God's eyes we are, in Christ, when we hide our life in him. When God looks at us he sees Christ's perfect righteousness instead of our faulty record.

> But now apart from the law the righteousness of God has been made known, to which the Law and the Prophets testify. This righteousness is given through faith in Jesus Christ to all who believe. There is no difference between Jew and Gentile, for

all have sinned and fall short of the glory of God, and all are justified freely by his grace through the redemption that came by Christ Jesus. (Romans 3:21–24)

Acceptance with God is not something we earn or deserve. We are *justified freely by his grace.*

Therefore, since we have been justified through faith, we have peace with God through our Lord Jesus Christ, through whom we have gained access by faith into this grace in which we now stand. (Romans 5:1–2)

When we are justified we have *peace.* Until we accept the gospel we are restless and insecure deep in our souls. We all long for acceptance with God. When we have it, and not until we have it, we have true peace, *peace with God.*

This is what the Protestant reformer, Martin Luther, had to say about the doctrine of justification:

[Justification by faith] is. . . the principal article of all Christian doctrine. . . Most necessary it is. . . that we should know this article well, teach it unto others, and beat it into their heads continually.[13]

In other places he called it the "chief."

The "chief," the "chiefest," and "the most principal and special article of Christian doctrine," "for this doctrine maketh true Christians indeed." In fact, he said, "if the article of justification be once lost, then is all true Christian doctrine lost."[14]

Justification was the key word and central teaching of the Protestant Reformation—which was the great return to the New Testament gospel of grace. Justification simply means to be accepted by God, to be put right with him. Sometimes justification has been defined as "just as if I never sinned" because that is how God views me when I hide my life in Christ. But really that definition is insufficient and can even be misleading. Justification does mean that, but it means more: even though I still sin I am still accepted by God in Christ.

In Galatians 2:16 two kinds of justification are contrasted. Three times Paul declares we are not justified by *observing the law*. You can never gain acceptance with God by observing the law, any law. I agree with Luther when he writes: This refers to *the work of the whole law, whether it be judicial, ceremonial, or moral.*[15]

The law can never justify, for that is not its purpose. The law just points out we are sinners in need of a savior. These Scriptures reveal our utter need for a savior:

> Now we know that whatever the law says, it says to those who are under the law, so that every mouth may be silenced and the whole world held accountable to God. Therefore no one will be declared righteous in God's sight by the works of the law; rather, through the law we become conscious of our sin. (Romans 3:19–20)

The law points out sin, but it cannot do anything to fix the problem, as Paul points out: "So the law was our guardian until Christ came that we might be justified by faith. Now that this faith has come, we are no longer under a guardian" (Galatians 3:24–25).

The law reveals the holiness of God, the sinfulness of humans, and the desperate need of a savior. The law drives us to the Savior, then its work is done.

In Galatians 2:16 we are told three times we are not justified by observing the law. Instead, we are told three times we are justified *by faith in Jesus Christ*. To say we are justified by faith does not mean we contribute to our salvation by our faith, since salvation is totally dependent on God's loving initiative in Christ. Rather, we receive by faith what has already been provided for us. Yes, we must take hold of it by faith, but faith is not a work. Even faith is a gift from God (Romans 12:3 says God has given each person a measure of faith). It is not actually faith that saves us, it is God, because of his love and grace. The phrase "saved by faith" is not in the Bible. When Christians talk about being saved by faith, many are just using that as an abbreviation. We are saved by God's grace, through faith. That's what *justified by faith* means.

Think of it this way. Suppose you were up in the mountains rock climbing and you slipped and fell down the cliff until you landed on a ledge. There is no way out, no way for you to save yourself. You must wait and wait and are ready to despair when you feel something touch your head. Someone spotted you from below and has hiked around and dropped a rope for you. You immediately grasp the rope in sheer relief and are pulled to safety. You are saved.

What is going to happen when you get to the top? Are you going to shake hands with your rescuer and say, "Let's congratulate each other because *we* saved me?" No, of course not! You were not the source of your salvation at all. You could have refused it, but if you had not grabbed that rope, you would be dead. If there was no rope, there would have been no salvation. To be justified by faith in Jesus Christ means we place our full confidence in him and trust him alone for our salvation.

REFLECTION

What does "justification" mean to me?

What is the difference between "saved by faith" and "saved by grace through faith"?

DAY 16

NEW LIFE

Whenever Paul spoke of justification by faith and contrasted it with the law, the legalists made accusations against him. For example, they would say, "Paul, if you put aside the law people are going to just go out and start sinning." Paul always had to anticipate the coming arguments, and in the closing verses of Galatians 2, he makes three points regarding what justification by faith means and does not mean:

BELIEVERS DO NOT LIVE IMMORAL LIVES

"But if, in seeking to be justified in Christ, we Jews find ourselves also among the sinners, doesn't that mean that Christ promotes sin? Absolutely not" (Galatians 2:17). Whenever Paul was charged with encouraging sin by preaching grace he always responded with an aggressive denial—"absolutely not!" he'd say.

Commenting on this verse John Stott writes:

Paul now proceeds to refute his critics' argument. Their charge that justification by faith encouraged a continuance in sin was ludicrous. They grossly misunderstood the gospel of justification. Justification is not a legal fiction, in which a man's status is changed, while his character is left untouched . . . Someone who is united to Christ is never the same person again. Instead, he is changed. It is not just his standing before God which has changed; it is he himself. . . he has become a new creation and begun a new life.[16]

Christ followers do not live unrepentant immoral lives, but it is not the law that keeps us from immorality. The law is not the highest definition of morality for New Covenant Christians. In fact:

BELIEVERS NO LONGER DEPEND ON THE LAW FOR MORAL GUIDANCE

"If I rebuild what I destroyed, then I really would be a lawbreaker. For through the law I died to the law so that I might live for God" (Galatians 2:18–19). Paul says if I go back under the law I just prove I am a lawbreaker because no one can keep it perfectly no matter how hard they try. Remember, this is in the context of Paul's discussion with Peter. When Peter pulled back and stopped eating with the Gentiles he was rebuilding the dividing barrier destroyed through the establishment of the New Covenant of grace, proving himself a lawbreaker by going back under the condemning force of the law.

Paul says, *through the law I died to the law.* You can never find acceptance with God through the law, only condemnation; going back under it after being justified proves you a sinner under its condemning glare. But when you die to the law, you are freed to live a new life for God. In that new life of liberty, believers depend on the Holy Spirit as a moral guide rather than the law. Galatians 5 will make that much clearer for us: "But if you are led by the Spirit, you are not under the law" (verse 18). When we are justified by faith we do not live immoral lives, not because the law is our moral guide, but because:

BELIEVERS ARE GRANTED A NEW LIFE, BY FAITH IN CHRIST, MOTIVATED BY HIS LOVING GIFT

> I have been crucified with Christ and I no longer live, but Christ lives in me. The life I now live in the body, I live by faith in the Son of God, who loved me and gave himself for me. (Galatians 2:20)

Notice this text speaks of a new life believers live: *the life I now live.* When we are justified by faith, we become united with Christ. When we are united with Christ, then his death becomes our death, and his resurrection becomes our resurrection; we were with him at the cross because he was our representative. And now, by faith, the risen Christ lives in us through his Spirit. The new life we live as Christ followers, gradually being transformed more and more into the image of Christ, is really not our own doing, but Christ living his life through us.

What motivates us to live this new life? Is it the law which says, "don't do this" or "don't do that"? Absolutely not! We are motivated to live by faith in Jesus because he *loved us and gave himself for us.* Do you see that in the text? The motive for a life of loving obedience to God is the fact that Jesus first loved us and gave himself for us. It is the cross that motivates us to live in a way that expresses thankfulness to God; that is what the Christian life is—a "Thank You Life," working from victory, not toward victory, responding to God's grace, grateful for the cross. *I live by faith in the Son of God, who loved me and gave himself for me.*

My mentor, Dr. Richard Fredericks, once told me his mentor used to say, "The gospel is like a diamond. Keep holding it up in the light and turning it; more and more glory will stream forth." The more you appreciate the love of God as seen at the cross, the more it changes you.

Paul concludes this section by saying, "I do not set aside the grace of God, for if righteousness could be gained through the law, Christ died for nothing" (Galatians 2:21).

False teachers may have accused him of setting aside the grace of God by teaching that the age of the law was over, but in reality, he was establishing the grace of God. Unlike Peter, who temporarily set aside grace in favor of law, Paul says, *I do not set aside the grace of God.* He remained steadfastly determined to hold to the gospel of grace, and here's why: if it was possible to gain favor with God by the law, *Christ died for nothing!*

Those are strong words. If we hold to a theology that says other things must be added to the gospel for salvation then we are in reality saying Christ's death was insufficient!

Please understand Christ's death is all-sufficient. You cannot add to it or subtract from it. His finished accomplishment at Calvary's cross is all-sufficient. I choose to stake my life on that, choosing to trust him and him alone for salvation, rejoicing in the good news that I am accepted by God in Christ, and thanking him for the new life of peace, assurance, and freedom, and that comes by living in vital union with the risen Christ through his Spirit. I hope you feel the way I do.

REFLECTION

When have I wrestled with the idea that emphasizing grace might lead people to think they can live any way they please?

How does grace become a more powerful motivator than law in the life of a believer?

DAY 17

WHO HAS BEWITCHED YOU?

Let us start with a question: Why are some Christ followers led astray by false teaching? There were over 900 Bible–reading Christians who took part in the Jim Jones mass suicide in 1978. Seventy-nine people who believed in Jesus went up in flames with David Koresh in Waco, Texas, in 1993. Thirty-nine people, believing God was leading them through Scripture, thought they could catch a ride on a comet and enter Heaven's Gate after taking their own lives in 1997.

Those are extreme examples. There are more respectable groups, some labeled as cults and some not, that are well and thriving today who hold to various false teachings such as the following: you can save dead people by getting baptized for them; books besides the Bible contain material as authoritative and binding as the Bible; Jesus wasn't divine; the Holy Spirit isn't a separate entity from the Father and Son; you should never go to a doctor if you are sick; it is a sin to take a blood transfusion;

snake handling should be a part of worship services; Christians must use God's Hebrew names; you must speak in unknown tongues to be saved; some people will be saved or lost because of what day they worship on; Christians must keep all the Jewish feast days; using birth control is a sin; what God reveals to people individually has equal or greater authority than the Bible; we can predict how and when the final events of history will happen by watching what happens in Israel; every Christian who truly has faith will be healthy and wealthy; you can advertise a miracle service and guarantee God will show up and do miracles on command; only one denomination is the true church. . . and that list could go on and on.

Why are some Christ followers led astray by false teaching? I think one reason is many believers are not grounded in Scripture and have not learned to use the Bible responsibly, study it diligently, and apply it properly. Therefore, they are "tossed back and forth by the waves, and blown here and there by every wind of teaching and by the cunning and craftiness of men" (Ephesians 4:14). Believers do well to follow the example of the Bereans described as people who "examined the Scriptures every day to see if what Paul said was true" (Acts 17:11).

When we examine the Scriptures we must do it responsibly because the Bible can be made to say just about anything with a proof–text approach. Every one of the false teachings I listed above have Bible verses people use to support them. For those who are seeking to learn how to study the Bible in a responsible way, I often recommend the excellent book: *How to Read the Bible for all its Worth* by Gordon Fee and Douglas Stuart.[17]

Another reason Christians are sometimes led astray by false teaching is "the flesh." Our flesh, our natural human nature, is drawn toward religious systems that make us look good and feature what we can do. Rather than depending on what God has already done for us in Christ, there is a human tendency for us to want to add to his accomplishment, or improve on it, or finish it ourselves. Unless it is constantly checked, there is a natural drift toward some kind of legalistic, works–oriented religion. Cults and variant groups appeal to the flesh—the notion that you can do something or believe something everyone else is missing, and thus be a part of the chosen few.

A man who attended Grace Place for a while really got excited about the good news of the gospel—that salvation is a free gift, received through faith because of God's grace. For some time he rejoiced in his newfound freedom in Christ, but then some legalists got a hold of him and started working on him. They presented fear–based arguments that made him start worrying again about his salvation. They suggested he was being deceived at Grace Place, urging him to read a book written by a paranoid conspiracy–type legalist who sees anyone who talks about grace as someone who is promoting a careless lifestyle. This good man got confused, pressured from friends and family, and finally decided to go back into legalism—a Christ–plus–something gospel. Immediately he lost his joy.

I feel like echoing Paul, saying, "You foolish people, who has bewitched you?" I can understand some of what Paul was feeling when he said those very words to some Christians who had lost their joy and gone back to Old Covenant bondage: "You foolish Galatians! Who has bewitched you? Before your very eyes Jesus Christ was clearly portrayed as crucified" (Galatians 3:1).

Paul calls the Galatians *foolish* because they turned away from the gospel of grace alone to a Christ–plus–something version (which is really no gospel at all). By *foolish* he does not mean they are dumb; he is saying they are behaving in an unwise manner. The Greek word for foolish means "to not use understanding, to not apply the mind, to act in a senseless way." Jesus used the same word when he spoke to a couple disciples on the road to Emmaus who had misunderstood the cross and empty tomb. He said, "How foolish you are, and how slow of heart to believe all that the prophets have spoken!" (Luke 24:25). They were *foolish* because they failed to see what was right in front of them, and they failed to apply what they already knew.

So it was with the Galatians. It was as though they had become hypnotized, *bewitched*. The word means "fascinated by false representations." It was like they had been placed in a trance. They were slipping back into legalism even though they had seen the cross vividly. Paul reminds them: "Before your very eyes Jesus Christ was clearly portrayed as crucified." What does that mean? Had they actually witnessed the crucifixion? No, but Paul's preaching was centered in the cross. He had so clearly represented what Christ accomplished on Calvary's cross, no one could escape the reality of the message. When Paul preached it was as though they could hear the hammers clink, see the blood flow, and feel the angry crowd.

Literally the text says Jesus was "placarded" before them as crucified. In other words, there was no way anyone could miss the fact that the cross was the center of the gospel. It was as though Paul put a giant billboard in front of them. Jesus Christ and him crucified was always the heart of Paul's preaching; there was simply no way for anyone to miss it. He boldly proclaims, "May I never boast except in the cross of our Lord Jesus Christ, through which the world has been crucified to me, and I to the world" (Galatians 6:14).

I love the way John Stott summarizes the gospel:

The gospel is Christ crucified, His finished work on the cross. And to preach the gospel is publicly to portray Christ as crucified. The gospel is not good news primarily of a baby in a manger, a young man at a carpenter's bench, a preacher in the fields of Galilee, or even an empty tomb. The gospel concerns Christ upon His cross. . . This then is the gospel. It is not a general instruction about the Jesus of history, but

a specific proclamation of Jesus Christ crucified. . . Sinners
may be justified before God and by God, not because of any
works of their own, but because of the atoning work of Christ;
not because of anything that they have done or could do, but
because of what Christ did once, when He died. The gospel is
not good advice to men, but good news about Christ; not an
invitation to us to do anything, but a declaration of what God
has done; not a demand, but an offer.[18]

This is what had been presented to the Galatians: Christ crucified
for them. They had understood the meaning of the cross, that Jesus had
taken their place and finished the work of salvation, and their hearts had
been moved; they had responded to the gospel. That is why Paul was so
amazed they were deserting. When you have clearly seen and understood
the cross, how can you go back to the bondage of a works–oriented
approach? It does not make sense. Paul would call that *foolish*!

REFLECTION

What examples have I seen of myself or others getting
influenced by cultic thinking?

When have I found my joy robbed by getting sucked
into works–oriented religious thinking and behavior?

WHAT DOES EXPERIENCE TEACH YOU?

P aul has already stated his premise that we are "justified by faith in Jesus Christ, not be observing the law" (Galatians 2:16). He now goes on to defend his premise with two lines of argument: experience and Scripture.

First, he appeals to their own experience when they were converted, and then he moves to what the Scriptures teach about salvation through faith. These two arguments are not presented in order of priority. God's Word always takes priority over what your experience tells you, but to get things started, Paul appeals first to the Galatians' own experience in verses 2–5 with a series of rhetorical questions, starting with "I would like to learn just one thing from you: Did you receive the Spirit by the works of the law, or by believing what you heard?" (Galatians 3:2).

These words, *I would like to learn just one thing from you,* might sound a bit snarky, but this was a common form of debate in those days, applying strong language and rhetorical questions in order to present a logical argument. His basic question here is: How did you get started as Christians? By faith or by observing the law? The question would be immediately obvious to the listeners since the Gentiles in Galatia had not even been instructed about the law until after their conversion when the Judaizers showed up. It was obvious; they had believed, been converted, and received the Holy Spirit by faith.

Two things happen when you believe the gospel and receive Christ. First, you are justified, you are accepted by God, and made right with him. Your sins are all pardoned, and you are supplied with Christ's righteousness.

Pretend you owed someone $10 million. You must pay or go to prison. Even if you could arrange a payment plan of $40,000 per year it would take 250 years to pay it off. You are condemned and hopeless. But then someone stands up in court and says, "I'll take care of it." Instantly, you are pardoned and forgiven the entire debt. Wouldn't that be wonderful? You walk out of the courtroom filled with joy. You are free. Let's suppose you discover this person had not only paid your debt but had also at the same time deposited $20 million in an account under your name. That is what happens when you are justified by faith. Jesus not only forgives all your sins, but covers your account with his righteousness. That is the first thing that happens at conversion. Then second, you are given the Holy Spirit. Instead of just being an outside influencer, leading you to Christ, the Holy Spirit now comes into your life, bringing confirmation you are a child of God, empowering you to serve God, and leading you to live a life that honors God.

What is Paul referring to when he speaks of the Galatians "receiving" the Spirit? Some people teach the Holy Spirit comes later after conversion as a second blessing. Those who hold this view cite some examples in the book of Acts. They insist the reception of the Holy Spirit is always accompanied by supernatural evidence, such as speaking in tongues, and that it happens sometime after conversion. I do not believe that is what the Bible teaches, but rather we receive the Spirit when we are saved, and he brings confirmation we are God's children. When you become God's child, you receive his Spirit: "Because you are his sons, God sent the Spirit of his Son into our hearts, the Spirit who calls out, 'Abba, Father'" (Galatians 4:6).

The Spirit brings confirmation that we are God's children:

The Spirit you received does not make you slaves, so that you live in fear again; rather, the Spirit you received brought about your adoption to sonship. And by him we cry, "Abba, Father." The Spirit himself testifies with our spirit that we are God's children. (Romans 8:15–16)

When you believe the gospel, God's Spirit comes into your life and seals you and guarantees your inheritance:

And you also were included in Christ when you heard the message of truth, the gospel of your salvation. When you believed, you were marked in him with a seal, the promised Holy Spirit, who is a deposit guaranteeing our inheritance until the redemption of those who are God's possession—to the praise of his glory. (Ephesians 1:13–14)

Paul reminds the Galatians they were saved and received the Spirit by faith (not by works). At that point the Judaizers might have said, "Okay, okay, faith gets you in, but obedience to the law keeps you in." Paul seems to anticipate that response as he continues the rhetorical questions: "Are you so foolish? After beginning by means of the Spirit, are you now trying to finish by means of the flesh?" (Galatians 3:3).

His main point is you stay right with God the same way you get right with God: it is all by faith from beginning to end. When the apostle writes, "are you now trying to finish by means of the flesh?" he is using the word *flesh* to refer to human effort. "Are you going to try to finish with human effort what you started in the Spirit?" (Paul will have a lot to say about the contrast between Spirit and flesh in chapter 5. He sets up the contrast here).

Paul talks about trying to *finish* by means of the flesh. The Greek word can also be translated "accomplish, perfect, complete." It is the same word used in Philippians 1:6 where Paul declares the one who started the work in your life will complete it himself: "Being confident of this, that he who began a good work in you will carry it on to completion until the day of Christ Jesus" (Philippians 1:6).

What a great promise! The answer to Paul's rhetorical question in Galatians 1:3 is you stay right with God the same way you got right with God: by faith alone, not faith plus works. As Paul continues to remind the Galatians of their experience he asks another question: "Have you experienced so much in vain—if it really was in vain?" (Galatians 3:4).

The word for *experienced* can also be translated "suffered." Whenever you take a stand for the gospel, there will usually be some legalist who persecutes you. Maybe some of you know from experience. I sure do. When I was leaving a legalistic system, there was a professor who published papers condemning me. People tried to discredit me, and to this day there is a dishonest anonymous blogger who has written slanderous things about me, trying to make it appear that because I teach grace, I also promote an "anything goes" philosophy for myself and others.

Whenever you take a stand for the gospel, some legalist will persecute you. Paul says to the believers in Galatia: "Why would you want to suffer for the gospel and then go back to legalism and thus prove the persecutors right after all?"

Paul suffered in taking the gospel throughout the Roman Empire. He and his traveling companions were misrepresented, threatened, abused, chased out of places, even stoned and left for dead, and this persecution was coming from God–fearing Jews, not pagans. The new Christians of Galatia must have also experienced some of that abuse for the sake of the gospel. When Paul and Barnabas circled back through those cities, they went about "strengthening the disciples and encouraging them to remain true to the faith. . . through many hardships" (Acts 14:22).

Paul appeals to those heading into legalism and says, "Do not rob your suffering of its meaning and prove the legalists right in persecuting you!" To punch home his point, Paul raises one more question before turning to Scriptural support: "So again I ask, does God give you his Spirit and work miracles among you by the works of the law, or by your believing what you heard?" (Galatians 3:5).

This question is basically a restatement of an earlier one. The only thing new is the mention of *miracles*. The Greek word translated "miracles" here is *dunamis* which means power (we get our word "dynamite" from this word). When you come to Christ he displays his power in your life. Every conversion is a miracle, and miracles happen through the Spirit, not because you observe the law, but because you believe the gospel.

In verses 1–5 Paul appeals to experience. If you are a believer and you are ever tempted to resort to a life of legalism, reflect on your experience. Recall the freedom and joy you first found when you accepted the gospel of grace, trusting completely in Christ's finished work.

REFLECTION

Have I considered and accepted the fact that the Holy Spirit of God is in me as a believer and that he wants to bring inner confirmation and assurance I am a child of God?

Have I or someone I know experienced attacks or suffered in some way because of the gospel?

DAY 19

WHAT DOES SCRIPTURE TEACH YOU?

Do not forget your experience. But do not stop there. Take your stand on the clear teaching of the Word of God. This is where Paul moves in verses 6–9, presenting the argument of justification by faith from the Hebrew Scriptures when he writes, "So also Abraham believed God, and it was credited to him as righteousness" (Galatians 3:6).

The Judaizers were big fans of Moses, constantly saying, "Moses said do this, Moses said do that." Paul argues, "Let us do better than that. You want to go back in time? Okay, let us go back past Moses to Abraham; after all, he was the original father of the Jews, and let us think about what really happened back there, all of you who want to be called 'children of Abraham.'"

He quotes a verse from Genesis 15 where God promised to bless the nations through Abraham. Even in his old age, God asked him to try to count the starts and then informed Abraham his descendants would be like that in number, and Abraham chose to believe God. The text says because he believed God and righteousness was *credited* to him. He received a good credit rating.

You've probably received those tantalizing notices in the mail advertising a new credit card: "Pre–approved Credit. Immediate Acceptance." A bank somewhere is assuming that you will pay your debts (along with substantial interest, they hope), so they are eager to extend you credit.

The gospel is totally different because it offers you "righteousness credit" based on Jesus Christ and his faithfulness. It is based on God's promise to pay, not ours. We could never credit enough to our account if we were dependent on our own righteousness, so God says, "Just believe and I will pay the bill." You have immediate acceptance with pre–approved credit based on *Christ's* credit rating, not yours.

Abraham was saved by faith. That is the only way anyone can ever be saved—before the cross or after the cross. He looked ahead by faith to God's provision; we look back by faith. When we believe, we become spiritual children of Abraham: "Understand, then, that those who have faith are children of Abraham" (Galatians 3:7).

There is a lot of confusion in the church today about this. Many people are focusing on literal Israel thinking that is where God's primary activity is going on—the physical children of Abraham. But God's primary activity is going on through his church, his bride, his body. The church is made up of all the spiritual children of Abraham—those who believe the gospel.

What makes you a child of Abraham? It is belonging to Christ, which happens when you believe the gospel, when you lay hold by faith of God's gift of grace in Christ. "If you belong to Christ, then you are Abraham's seed, and heirs according to the promise" (Galatians 3:29).

Now go back to verse 8. "Scripture foresaw that God would justify the Gentiles by faith, and announced the gospel in advance to Abraham: 'All nations will be blessed through you'" (Galatians 3:8).

God *announced the gospel in advance*. Abraham was saved by the gospel even though he lived before it was accomplished at Calvary's cross. God announced it in advance by promising to bless all nations through Abraham. Jesus Christ would later be born as a descendant of Abraham and the fulfillment of the promise, blessing with salvation all who would receive the gift through faith: "So those who rely on faith are blessed along with Abraham, the man of faith" (Galatians 3:9).

God's method of salvation has always been through faith. The law was a temporary measure which pointed out sin and the need for a savior, but never a method of salvation. Paul hammers away at his point, that from beginning to end, justification is by faith, not by works, not through observing the law; we are saved by faith alone, not faith plus works.

We have done some heavy theological plowing through the text. Now let me make things crystal clear. Allow me to tell you what I encourage you to know and what I encourage you to do as a result of this passage.

I want you to know two things. First, God loves you dearly. He planned for you to be his child long ago when he announced the gospel to Abraham, declaring the blessings of justification by faith would extend to you. You are a wanted child of a loving heavenly parent. Max Lucado wrote: "If God had a refrigerator, your picture would be on it. If He had a wallet, your photo would be in it. He sends you flowers every spring and a sunrise every morning... Face it, friend. He is crazy about you!"[19] Your heavenly father loves you dearly, ordaining you to be his child long ago. I want you to know that.

Second, if you are a believer, I want you to know and be assured God will complete the work in you that he began. God doesn't get things started and then back off. "Being confident of this, that he who began a good work in you will carry it on to completion until the day of Christ Jesus" (Philippians 1:6). Count on that, live each day the same way you started the Christian life—by faith. Be confident. Be assured. You are in good hands, and you are safe. Know that.

Now here's what I would invite you to do:

- Watch out for false teaching because it abounds. Be biblically grounded and keep the cross central. Do not go back to legalism if you have been delivered from it.
- Believe faith alone saves you and saves you to the end. It is one thing to know it and another to believe it. You stay right with God the same way you got right with God—by faith alone, not faith plus works.
- Live with confidence. Be confident, not in yourself for a minute, but in Christ. Paul said, "I boast in only one thing, in the cross of Christ." Live with confidence.
- Let somebody else know the good news. Do you really believe it? If so, it is a treasure to share with others!

REFLECTION

Am I confident God loves me dearly and will complete the work in me that he began? Why or why not?

What keeps me from having confidence or from sharing the good news with others?

DAY 20

THE LAW CANNOT SOLVE OUR PROBLEM

We live in an increasingly godless culture. Well–meaning citizens are looking for ways to improve our society. What is the answer? Could it be the Ten Commandments? After all, the Ten Commandments say very clearly not to kill, not to steal, not to commit adultery, etc. Maybe we need to put more emphasis on the law, find ways to display the commandments, keep them in front of our youth so they will know, respect, and obey God's law. School boards in several states have battled over initiatives to display the Ten Commandments on the walls in public school, and Christians with good intentions have promoted this as a way to instill God's values and curb the lawless behavior that is so rampant. A while ago, an Arkansas senator started a GoFundMe account with a goal to raise $16,000 to put up a Ten Commandments monument at the state capitol. Within days he raised over $18,000. Of course, soon atheists were protesting, and the Hindus and Satanists wanted a monument too. Are the Ten Commandments the answer? Will holding up the law solve our problems? If we just rely on the law more, will we be a better society? That is a good question, one to which the Bible provides a definitive answer.

> For all who rely on the works of the law are under a curse, as it is written: "Cursed is everyone who does not continue to do everything written in the Book of the Law." Clearly no one who relies on the law is justified before God, because "the righteous will live by faith." The law is not based on faith; on the contrary, it says, "The person who does these things will live by them." Christ redeemed us from the curse of the law by becoming a curse for us, for it is written: "Cursed is everyone who is hung on a pole." He redeemed us in order that the blessing given to Abraham might come to the Gentiles through Christ Jesus, so that by faith we might receive the promise of the Spirit. (Galatians 3:10–14)

Do these verses indicate the law is the answer? Will memorizing the Ten Commandments, or hanging them in public places, or placing them on monuments lead to a better society? No, the law is not the answer; the law can only point to the answer. In fact, relying on the law only brings a curse and condemnation.

> For all who rely on the works of the law are under a curse, as it is written: "Cursed is everyone who does not continue to do everything written in the Book of the Law." (Galatians 3:10)

Before we can interpret this passage we need to raise the question up front: What is the law? Is it the Ten Commandments? Is it the other laws God gave the Jews at Sinai through Moses? Is it the entire writings of Moses found in Exodus through Deuteronomy, which served as the basis of the covenant God made with Israel? The answer is "yes" to all of the above. The basis of God's covenant with Israel made at Sinai was the Ten Commandments, the summary of the covenant. The rest of the laws were amplification and application of the covenant. So, the law is summarized in the Big Ten but includes the entire law package: Exodus through Deuteronomy. All of it is the Law of Moses, and all of it is the law of God, one and the same.

Let me give you a few texts to establish this fact. The Ten Commandments were the basic covenant with Israel. The Ten Commandments were called *the words of the covenant*:

Moses was there with the Lord forty days and forty nights without eating bread or drinking water. And he wrote on the tablets the words of the covenant—the Ten Commandments. (Exodus 34:28)

What are the *words of the covenant*? The Big Ten. In Deuteronomy, the Ten Commandments are actually called the *covenant*: "[God] declared to you his covenant, the Ten Commandments, which he commanded you to follow and then wrote them on two stone tablets" (Deuteronomy 4:13).

The Ten Commandment law was God's basic covenant with Israel. Other laws were given as interpretation, expansion, and application, but the Ten were called the *words* of the covenant, and the additional regulations were called the *book* of the covenant or *the book of the law* (it means the same).

Then [Moses] took the Book of the Covenant and read it to the people. They responded, "We will do everything the LORD has said; we will obey." (Exodus 24:7)

"Take this Book of the Law and place it beside the ark of
the covenant of the LORD your God. There it will remain as a
witness against you." (Deuteronomy 31:26).

So the law was made up of both the *words* of the covenant and
the *book* of the covenant. And they were stored side by side in the Ark
of the Covenant, the same one Indiana Jones was looking for. It was
called Ark of the Covenant because it contained the covenant—both
the Ten Commandment summary (the *words*) and the more detailed
explanations and interpretations (the *book*)—all of it was the covenant,
and all of it was the law.

You might be wondering why we are taking time with these details.
This is important foundation for understanding the message of Galatians,
the heart of which we are getting into in Galatians 3–4.

The law contained both moral principles as eternal as God himself,
and it also contained ceremonial, ritual features—some of them serving
to separate Israel from the other nations, some of them pointing as
shadows and types toward fulfillment in Christ, the Messiah. Both
elements—moral principles and ceremonial aspects—are contained in
the Ten Commandments as well as throughout the rest of the law.

Sometimes people have gotten the impression the Ten
Commandments are God's moral law and the rest was a temporary
ceremonial package. This view assumes there is a clear distinction
between the moral and ceremonial laws within the Law of Moses. Some
have even gone so far as to call the Ten Commandments the Law of God
and the other laws the Law of Moses.

That view presents a big problem though because the Scriptures
do not support it. The totality of God's laws for Israel are spoken of
repeatedly as the Law of God. The Law of God and the Law of Moses
are the same thing, one package, and both moral and ceremonial aspects
are intermingled constantly throughout the entire law.

The Bible never gives the impression the Ten Commandments were 100 percent moral laws which are eternal and the rest of the Mosaic laws are secondary and temporary ceremonial laws. In fact, both elements—moral principles and ceremonial aspects—are present in the Ten Commandments as well as throughout the rest of the law.

If you read carefully the Ten Commandments you'll notice in the fourth and tenth commandments are references to *slaves* (certainly not an eternal, moral principle); in the fifth commandment there is a promise about *land* related specifically to Israel in Canaan. These aspects of the Ten Commandments are neither eternal nor moral principles.

Another ceremonial aspect in the Ten Commandments is the Sabbath. We will study this more carefully when we get to Galatians 4, but the Sabbath was declared by God to be a special *sign* of the covenant for Israel (Exodus 31:13). In Leviticus 23 the Sabbath is listed alongside (as equal to) a host of other ceremonial holy days and feasts that pointed to Christ and were called *shadows* fulfilled in Christ, the substance (Colossians 2:16–17).

Just as the Ten Commandments were a mixture of moral principles and ceremonial aspects so with the rest of the law. When Jesus was asked about the greatest commandments (Matthew 22:36–40) he responded by quoting two commandments from the Law of Moses which were not a part of the Ten:

1. Love God with all your heart, soul, and strength—
    Deuteronomy 6:5
2. Love your neighbor as yourself—Leviticus 19:18

That second command is a moral principle which is restated by Jesus as the heart of the New Covenant, but in Leviticus 19 it is right in the context of countless temporary ceremonial laws specific to Israel, and the very next verse is a law about not mixing two kinds of material in clothing.

Here is the point I want you to understand and remember as we go through the rest of Galatians. God's law, given to Israel at Sinai, was the basis of his covenant with Israel. It contained both eternal, moral principles and temporary, ceremonial aspects which set Israel apart from the other nations or pointed to the coming Messiah. The law was given by God, but it was never intended to be his supreme revelation. What was his supreme revelation? Jesus Christ.

> In the past God spoke to our ancestors through the prophets at many times and in various ways, but in these last days he has spoken to us by his Son, whom he appointed heir of all things, and through whom also he made the universe. The Son is the radiance of God's glory and the exact representation of his being. (Hebrews 1:1–3)

What is the supreme revelation of God's character, *the exact representation of his being*? The law? No, the Son, Jesus. Now that Jesus has come and revealed the gospel in its fullness, this side of the glorious cross, New Covenant Christians look to Jesus, not the law.

The ceremonial aspects of the law have passed away. All the eternal moral principles of the law are restated in the New Testament and continue as God's expectations, but we are not motivated by the law. The Spirit of God lives in our hearts to motivate and guide us to fulfill God's will, and we are only able to live for God because we have been released from the penalty and condemnation of the law through Christ.

You see, Jesus accomplished all the law required and fulfilled, all the law promised. He kept the moral principles of the law perfectly (unlike any other human on this planet), and he fulfilled every ceremonial aspect that pointed to him. What is more, he abolished the law as a dividing wall between Jews and Gentiles, thus removing the separation aspect of the law.

The moral principles of the law cannot help us out, instead, they only condemn us. None of us can keep the law perfectly. The Pharisees in Christ's time thought they were doing all right. "We keep the law," they boasted. In the Sermon on the Mount (Matthew 5–7), Jesus said, in essence, "Oh, yeah, you think you have never murdered? Think again. Have you hated someone? You think you have never committed adultery? But have you ever thought about it? If so, then you broke the law. Here is the standard: 'Be perfect even as your Father in heaven!'" In other words, Jesus showed them no one can truly keep the law. Yes, it remains as a standard, but it is unreachable.

So, the law cannot solve our sin problem. It has an important function, though. It shows us we are sinners in need of a Savior. It puts us under a curse of condemnation, which drives us to seek a solution for our guilt. And there is only one solution—the One who took the curse for us.

REFLECTION

Why doesn't posting the Ten Commandments on a wall prevent people from sinning?

What does this statement mean to me: "Jesus accomplished all that the law required and fulfilled all the law promised"?

DAY 21

REDEEMED
FROM THE CURSE

I n the last chapter we saw clearly that the law cannot save us or solve
our sin problem, instead, it puts us under a curse of condemnation.

> For all who rely on the works of the law are under a curse, as
> it is written: "Cursed is everyone who does not continue to do
> everything written in the Book of the Law." (Galatians 3:10)

In the verses just before this Paul established that justification by
faith, apart from the law, was the only way anyone could be right with
God. He used the Old Testament Scriptures and the story of Abraham to
prove it. Now he uses the Scriptures to show it was never God's intention
for people to be made right by the law. The law is limited in what it can
accomplish; the law brings a *curse*. Why? Because it points out sin and
condemns those who do not obey.

The apostle quotes from Deuteronomy 27:26 to establish his point.
When the Old Covenant was read originally, a series of blessings for

obedience and curses for disobedience were pronounced. The last of the curses was "cursed is everyone who does not do everything written in the Book of the Law." The law required obedience to everything. James wrote, "Whoever keeps the whole law and yet stumbles at just one point is guilty of breaking all of it" James 2:10. Paul agreed when he wrote, "Every man who lets himself be circumcised. . . is obligated to obey the whole law" (Galatians 5:3). He is speaking about those who insisted on circumcision for religious reasons as the entry sign of the Old Covenant.

If you tie your boat to the dock with a chain, it will only be as secure as the weakest link in the chain. If a raging storm causes even one link to break, the boat breaks away. The same is true of those who try to come to God based on their own perfection. They must measure up in every specific or they will be shipwrecked. Guess what? It cannot be done. Please do not be deceived. Do not try relying on your performance either to get right with God or to stay right with him. The law is good and holy, but it cannot make us good and holy, for it only shows us how sinful we are and puts us under a curse by condemning us to death for our disobedience.

You might ask why God gave us the law then. The simple answer is he loves us. What would you think of a doctor who knows you have a deadly but curable disease, yet refuses to tell you about the cure? Not a very nice doctor, right? Why then do people get mad at God when he diagnoses our sin problem for us?

The law is an important tool God uses to diagnose sin. Paul says: I would never have come to know sin except through the Law (Romans 7:7). Look what Paul says about the law in another place:

> We know that the law is good if one uses it properly. We also know that the law is made not for the righteous but for lawbreakers and rebels, the ungodly and sinful, the unholy and irreligious, for those who kill their fathers or mothers,

for murderers, for the sexually immoral, for those practicing
homosexuality, for slave traders and liars and perjurers—
and for whatever else is contrary to the sound doctrine that
conforms to the gospel concerning the glory of the blessed
God, which he entrusted to me. (1 Timothy 1:8–11)

Who is the law for? The *righteous*? No. Who is it for? The *ungodly.*
Why does God want to point out the sin of the ungodly? Because he
loves them dearly and does not want to see them perish in their sins (2
Peter 3:9). The purpose of the law is to show us our sinfulness not to
keep us from sin (it cannot do that), or to clean us up (it cannot do that
either), but to drive us to the cure.

Do not get mad at God for pointing out your sin. He is a loving
God who is also an excellent physician with a perfect cure. The purpose
of the law is to lead us to Christ that we might be justified by faith
(Galatians 3:24). Jesus is our only answer.

"Clearly no one who relies on the law is justified before God,
because 'the righteous will live by faith'" (Galatians 3:11). Once again
Paul appeals to the Scriptures for support. This time he quotes from
Habakkuk 2:4, *the righteous shall live by faith.* No person in any generation
has been able to meet God's standards of perfect righteousness by trying
hard or by obedience to the law. It has never happened, and it will never
happen. We can only be counted righteous by accepting his provision
by faith.

Do not get the impression that after we are accepted by God by
faith, we must *continue* to be accepted by him through obedience to
the law. We humans always want to come up with some kind of system
where we get some of the credit, but law and faith are incompatible
systems. They are not both/and systems; they are either/or roads. "The
law is not based on faith; on the contrary, it says, 'The person who does
these things will live by them'" (Galatians 3:12).

The gospel is based on faith, not the law; God has always and only saved people by faith. The law was a temporary system that pointed out sin and the need for a savior, and it never saved anyone, only condemned. Again, Paul quotes from the Scriptures where God says, "The person who does these things will live by them" (Leviticus 18:5). The expectation of the law is that it will be kept, entirely and perfectly. Hypothetically, a person who exhibits perfect righteousness by continual obedience to the law might be okay with God. But that is only hypothetical. In this world of sin, where we are all born with sinful human natures as a consequence of Adam's sin, none of us can keep God's law, meaning all of us are under the curse of God's law and deserve only one thing— death, eternal separation from the holy God of the universe. That is all any of us deserve, whether we want to admit it or not. The only judge that matters has already declared it so. There is no hope, zero chance for any of us, except for God's intervention. "Christ redeemed us from the curse of the law by becoming a curse for us, for it is written: 'Cursed is everyone who is hung on a pole'" (Galatians 3:13).

How is that for good news? The Greek word translated *redeemed* was a word commonly used for buying a slave's freedom. Christ redeemed us, bought us back from our slavery to sin, purchased us by paying a price, the only price high enough to redeem all of humanity. We were redeemed "with the precious blood of Christ, a lamb without blemish or defect" (1 Peter 1:19). The only way Christ could break the curse was to take the curse, even become cursed by God. In fact, "God made him who had no sin to be sin for us, so that in him we might become the righteousness of God" (2 Corinthians 5:21). In a divine exchange Christ absorbed our curse and took it himself.

Again, Paul quotes from the Scriptures when he writes, "Anyone who is hung on a pole is under God's curse" (Deuteronomy 21:23). When someone in the days of the Old Covenant was executed as a criminal (usually by stoning), he would then be hung on a post or tree until sundown as a visible representation of condemnation by God. The person was not cursed because he was hanged on a tree, but he was hanged on a tree because he was cursed. That is what happened at the cross. Christ took our curse. As Peter wrote, "'He himself bore our sins' in his body on the cross" (1 Peter 2:24). The Jews knew hanging on a tree was a sign of being under the curse of God, so they used the crucifixion of Jesus as the ultimate proof he was not the promised Messiah. But the Christians turned it around and said, "You are missing the whole point. Yes, he was under the curse of God because in order for him to legitimately justify us it was necessary for him to take our curse, bear our condemnation, pay our penalty for sin." When Jesus cried out on the cross, "My God, my God, why have you forsaken me" (Matthew 27:46), he was experiencing divine displeasure with sin. He was suffering the penalty of separation from God you and I deserve but never have to face if we receive the free gift of salvation.

Notice two of the most beautiful words in all of Scripture in Galatians 3:13—"for us." Why did Christ become a curse? For us! He redeemed us, all of us. You do not have to live under the curse of the law anymore for Christ redeemed us and set us free by taking the curse himself. All you have to do is take hold by faith of his gift of grace.

> He redeemed us in order that the blessing given to Abraham might come to the Gentiles through Christ Jesus, so that by faith we might receive the promise of the Spirit. (Galatians 3:14)

Notice the twofold result of Christ's finished redemption. First, the dividing walls are down, the gospel is for all people, there is no distinction, *in order that the blessing given to Abraham might come to the Gentiles through Christ Jesus.* What is the blessing given to Abraham? It is justification by faith (verses 6–9, 28).

Second, believers in Christ are given the wonderful gift of the promised Holy Spirit. As we shall see, the Spirit brings confirmation that we are God's children (4:6–7) and produces good fruit in our lives (5:18, 22–23).

REFLECTION

What do the words "We know that the law is good if one uses it properly" (1 Timothy 1:8) mean to me?

How does it impact my life to know Christ became a *curse* for me?

DAY 22

THE PURPOSE
OF THE LAW

H ave you ever been in jail or prison? Hopefully not. I have never been in jail. (I did come close once as a teenager when I took a ride to the police station with a group of friends in the back of a paddy wagon for disturbing the peace.) But as a pastor visiting people, I have visited jails a few times, even a high security prison. There is something about being in a prison I will never forget. The *clank*. First, they checked me out, made me empty my pockets and go through the metal detector before I walked through a heavy sliding steel door and heard the sound. *Clank!* I will never forget it. Of course, that sound must be all the more ominous for someone who commits a crime, is caught, declared guilty, condemned, sentenced to death, and then locked up on death row. Scripture teaches that is what the Law of God does. It cannot save us. It cannot help us be better. It cannot clean us up. It cannot change our hearts. All it can do is put us under a curse by showing us we are guilty sinners deserving death. The sound of the law is a solid metal *clank* as it locks us up as prisoners.

In the last chapter we read, "Cursed is everyone who does not continue to do everything written in the Book of the Law" (Galatians 3:10). Since none of us has obeyed God's law perfectly and continually, all of us end up under its curse. You might say, "But what about those who don't know God's law? What about those who never went to church or read the Bible?" It does not matter whether or not you have actually read God's written code of law found in the books of Moses; you still find yourself under its curse. Why? Because God has written the basic moral principles of his law on the heart of every person.

> Indeed, when Gentiles, who do not have the law, do by nature things required by the law, they are a law for themselves, even though they do not have the law, since they show that the requirements of the law are written on their hearts, their consciences also bearing witness, and their thoughts now accusing, now even defending them. (Romans 2:14–15)

Jesus said the Holy Spirit works in the world to "convict the world of guilt in regard to sin and righteousness and judgment" (John 16:8). The Spirit convicts us of what is wrong (*sin*), what is right (*righteousness*), and what difference it makes (*judgment*). Whether we suppress that conviction or not, we all know we should not do certain things, like murder or steal. We know it, but just knowing wrong does not necessarily keep people from doing it. But they still know it.

We are born into this world with a sinful nature we inherit as a result of Adam and Eve, our original parents' sin. By the time we reach the age where we know right from wrong, we have already developed a pattern of self–serving behavior, or sin. No person on this planet can escape the verdict of "guilty" sinner, locked up as prisoners by the law we have transgressed. *Clank!* We cannot atone for our sins. We cannot do enough good works to cancel out our debt. We cannot buy our way out of prison. We cannot beg our way out. We cannot bust our way out. We are held captive, locked up, the *clank* of solid metal ringing in our ears. There is no hope for any of us. Except. Except we might be granted a pardon and acquittal. That can only happen, though, if atonement is made.

The good news of the gospel is "that Christ redeemed us from the curse of the law by becoming a curse for us" (Galatians 3:13). Christ absorbed our curse by taking it on himself as our sinless substitute. He hung in our place at Calvary's cross and cancelled the curse for all who will accept his offer of salvation by grace through faith in his atoning sacrifice. The God of the universe is a God of love. His method of dealing with his creatures has always been on the basis of grace. He has always had just one plan of salvation—by grace alone through faith alone, based on his loving initiative. That is why the gospel is called the "eternal gospel" (Revelation 14:6). Jesus is referred to as "the Lamb who was slain from the creation of the world" (Revelation 13:8) because the cross was anticipated long before it happened.

The temporary era of the law—which we now refer to as "the Old Covenant"—was not an alternative method of salvation. Whether people lived before the cross and anticipated it by faith or whether they live this side of the cross (no longer in the shadows, but in the full radiant glory), all people who are saved are saved the same way—because of God's grace, poured out in Christ and received by faith.

The "Old Covenant law" era was a temporary stretch of salvation history where God provided an object lesson to reveal the holiness of himself, severity of sin, and the absolute need for a savior. That point is made clear in our passage:

> Brothers and sisters, let me take an example from everyday life. Just as no one can set aside or add to a human covenant that has been duly established, so it is in this case. (Galatians 3:15)

In the first part of Galatians 3, Paul establishes salvation came to Abraham by faith when he trusted God, not through law or works of any kind. God announced the gospel in advance to Abraham by promising the same blessing he received (justification by faith) would be made available to all nations.

At this point, the Judaizers might have argued and responded: "Okay, Paul, we will grant you that Abraham was saved by faith apart from the law. The law had not come yet, but when it came, it came later; therefore, it is superior. It is the full and final revelation; God's promise to Abraham was only partial for it anticipated the coming law, which is God's ultimate revelation."

Paul seems to have anticipated such an argument, so he demonstrates the superiority of the promise given to Abraham over the law given to Moses. He says, "Let me illustrate with an example from everyday life." He goes on in verse 15 to talk about a human covenant. What he is describing here is not some kind of contract between two parties, but rather a last will and testament a person establishes. The word covenant here can be translated "will." Once a will is made it cannot be changed by anyone else, and when it has been ratified by the death of the one who made it, it is unalterable; it cannot be added to or subtracted from.

Suppose your wealthy great-grandmother passes away, and after the funeral all the grandkids gather to hear the will read. There is breathless anticipation. Maybe you wonder, "Did she divide her millions equally? How much will I get?" Now imagine you discover to your dismay she willed her entire estate to a charitable foundation for the protection and adoption of stray cats. Every penny! You would not be too happy, would you? But what could you do about it? Not a thing. Once a will is ratified it cannot be altered. Paul says, *so it is in this case.* He utilizes this kind of an illustration to say the promise God made to Abraham was not changed by the temporary era of the law.

> The promises were spoken to Abraham and to his seed.
> Scripture does not say "and to seeds," meaning many people,
> but "and to your seed," meaning one person, who is Christ.
> (Galatians 3:16)

Promises given to Abraham—promises of a son, a land, a nation, and a coming blessing for all nations—those promises transcended literal Israel. The promises would be fulfilled in Christ, the *seed* (singular). Just as Christ was anticipated in Genesis 3:15 when God promised Eve her *seed* would crush the serpent, so Christ was anticipated when a promise was made regarding Abraham's *seed* (See Genesis 12:7, 13:15, 24:7).

All of the Old Testament was pointing to Jesus the promised Messiah. When Jesus arrived, he was the fulfillment of all God's promises. "For no matter how many promises God has made, they are 'Yes' in Christ. And so through him the 'Amen' is spoken by us to the glory of God" (2 Corinthians 1:20). In Christ the promises are "Yes," "Amen," fulfilled. God's covenant promises are fulfilled to you personally when you are *in Christ*, when you belong to Christ and have hidden your life in his. "If you belong to Christ, then you are Abraham's seed, and heirs according to the promise" (Galatians 3:29).

Some Christians today think the main focus of the Bible is the literal nation of Israel. This view insists the covenant promises made in the Old Testament must be fulfilled to literal Israel eventually. I do not agree with this view. I believe the main focus of the Bible is Jesus Christ. He is the one who fulfills the prophecies of Scripture, and in him all the promises are *Yes*. Those who belong to him are the true, spiritual *Israel of God* (as the church is called in Galatians 6:16; compare to 3:29).

The Christian era is not a parenthesis in salvation history. Rather, the Old Covenant (the law era) was the parenthesis in history. What is Paul saying? He goes on to explain, "What I mean is this: The law, introduced 430 years later, does not set aside the covenant previously established by God and thus do away with the promise" (Galatians 3:17).

The law came a long time after the promise of justification by faith was given to Abraham. But the coming of the law did not revoke the original gospel promise, and that is what this verse is saying. The time of 430 years represents the time of the Egyptian captivity. God had told Abraham his descendants would be strangers in a country and enslaved for about 400 years (Genesis 15:13). Later we are told Moses led the Israelites out of Egypt after exactly 430 years (Exodus 12:40). This reference is meant to be representative of the time between the covenant made with Abraham and the Sinai law-covenant made with Moses and the children of Israel. Do not lose sight of the point Paul is making here. The temporary law-covenant made at Mt. Sinai did not supersede or revoke the faith-promise made to Abraham: "For if the inheritance depends on the law, then it no longer depends on the promise; but God in his grace gave it to Abraham through a promise" (Galatians 3:18).

Notice how the law and promise are presented here as either/or systems. It is not both/and, but either/or. You do not approach God and find favor with him by faith and also by works of the law. There is only one way to be accepted by God. Do you see the key word in that verse? *Grace*, the only way to be justified or accepted by God—by grace, received through faith in Christ. To Abraham God gave a promise (fulfilled in Christ). To Moses He gave the law (summarized in the Ten Commandments).

Martin Luther wrote:

These two things (as I often repeat), to wit, the law and the promise, must be diligently distinguished. For in time, in place, and in person, and generally in all other circumstances, they are separate as far asunder as heaven and earth. . . Unless

the gospel be plainly discerned from the law, the true Christian
doctrine cannot be kept sound and uncorrupted.[20]

Why did Luther insist on keeping the law and gospel separate?
What is the difference between them? John Stott states it well:

> In the promise to Abraham God said, "I will. . . I will. . .
> I will. . . "But in the law of Moses God said, "Thou shalt
> . . . thou shalt not. . . "The promise sets forth a religion of
> God—God's plan, God's grace, God's initiative. But the law
> sets forth a religion of man—man's duty, man's works, man's
> responsibility. The promise (standing for the grace of God)
> had only to be believed. But the law (standing for the works
> of men) had to be obeyed. God's dealings with Abraham
> were in the category of "promise", "grace", and "faith". But
> God's dealings with Moses were in the category of "law",
> "commandments" and "works".[21]

Paul's point is Christianity is an extension of the everlasting
grace covenant God made with Abraham. It is not connected to the
law covenant (contrary to what the false teachers were trying to
tell the Galatians). If that is true, one might logically ask, why then
did God give the law? In anticipation of that question, Paul raises it
himself:

> Why, then, was the law given at all? It was added because of
> transgressions until the Seed to whom the promise referred
> had come. The law was given through angels and entrusted
> to a mediator. A mediator, however, implies more than one
> party; but God is one. (Galatians 3:19–20)

What was the purpose of the law? *It was added because of transgressions.* The law was added to define sin. In other words, the law was added to point out sin and make sin a legal offense. One translation reads: The law "was added to make wrong-doing a legal offence" (Galatians 3:19 NEB). Paul elaborates on this idea throughout his epistle to the Romans: "Through the law comes the knowledge of sin" (Romans 3:20 NASB 1995). "Where there is no law there is no transgression" (Romans 4:15). "I would not have known what sin was had it not been for the law" (Romans 7:7). So the law's work was to expose sin and turn wrongdoing into transgression.

Years ago, I lived in a neighborhood where there were no speed limit signs, and I figured that meant to drive at your own risk, choosing what you think is a safe speed. One day I got pulled over for speeding and was informed that if the speed limit is not posted, the law in our town states that the limit is 25 mph. Because I did not know that, I felt my offense was neither a legal offense nor a transgression. Unfortunately, the officer did not agree and wrote me a ticket. Later, the town installed speed limit signs in our neighborhood. The law was added, and it turned the offense into a transgression.

Do you see what the law does? It points out sin and turns it into transgression. In addition to telling us the purpose of the law in Galatians 3:19–20, Paul also tells us two things about the nature of the law. It is inferior and temporary.

First, the law is inferior to the gospel. He makes this point by contrasting the way the law and the promise were given. The law was delivered through angels to Moses (*a mediator*) to Israel; the promise was given directly from God to Abraham.

Second, the law is temporary in its duration. The words *added* and *until* indicate a beginning and ending time for the era of the law. The written code of law was *added* 430 years after the promise was given and was intended to last *until the Seed to whom the promise referred had come,* that is, until the coming of Christ.

REFLECTION

Why do you think Martin Luther wrote "Unless the gospel be plainly discerned from the law, the true Christian doctrine cannot be kept sound and uncorrupted"?

How does understanding that the purpose of the law was to expose sin and turn wrongdoing into transgression help me see the difference between law and grace?

DAY 23

NO LONGER
UNDER LAW

Remember the reason the book of Galatians was written. False teachers were telling new believers they must keep the law of Moses including all of its boundary markers—circumcision, abstinence from unclean foods, observance of the Sabbath and other Jewish holy days, etc. But what they failed to see was that the Old Covenant was a temporary arrangement. It did not always exist. It was *added.* It was not to be everlasting but only *until* the Seed, Christ, would come and establish the New Covenant as the final and full revelation of the everlasting gospel. Some people are still confused about this today.

At this point in the discussion, Paul anticipated another objection, and so he raises and answers one more question:

> Is the law, therefore, opposed to the promises of God?
> Absolutely not! For if a law had been given that could impart
> life, then righteousness would certainly have come by the law.
> (Galatians 3:21)

If the purpose of the law had been another method of salvation, then the law would have been opposed to the promise—they would be two polar opposite ways to be accepted by God. But the law's purpose was never salvation, just the opposite. The purpose of the law was condemnation. Look at the next verse:

> But Scripture has locked up everything under the control of sin, so that what was promised, being given through faith in Jesus Christ, might be given to those who believe. (Galatians 3:22)

The law *locked up everything under the control of sin,* for the law declares every person in the world is a prisoner of sin, *locked up.* The law slams the door shut with a sickening *clank* and shouts "guilty," "condemned," "cursed," "sentenced," "judged." The law can't solve the sin problem. It can only point it out.

Do you have scales in your house? We have some in our bathroom. I get on them every morning. But I do not like them. They are very condemning. It is not their fault, they just tell the truth (do they ever!). After the weekend they inform me of how careful I need to be in the coming week. They never lie. They are brutally honest. Anyone who battles the bulge is likely to laugh along with Erma Bombeck who said, "I'm not going to tell you how much I weigh but when I measure my girth and then step on the scales, I should be a 90–foot redwood."[22] The scales cannot help me trim a few pounds. They only reveal that there is a problem. They just say "overweight, overweight." A little card pops out that reads "One at a time please!" And that is the way of the law—like a set of bathroom scales that never offers grace.

The law tells the truth. It says "unholy," "unjust," "selfish," "lustful," "greedy," "hateful," "proud," "guilty, guilty, guilty." "Scripture has shut up everyone under sin" (Galatians 3:22, NASB 1995). The door slams shut, *clank*. The law locks us up as guilty prisoners, but here is the good news: the purpose of the law is not to leave us in prison, but to drive us to the source of freedom, to Jesus Christ our redeemer. The text says *so that*—the purpose of the law is *so that* we would see our need of salvation and put our faith in Jesus.

The fact that the law condemns us all as sinners is not meant to lead us to despair, but to lead us to Jesus. I like the classic way Martin Luther expressed this point:

> The principal point. . . of the law. . . is to make men not better but worse; that is to say, it shows unto them their sin, that by the knowledge thereof they may be humbled, terrified, bruised and broken, and by this means may be driven to seek grace, and so to come to that blessed Seed—Jesus Christ.[23]

The purpose of the law is to lead us to Christ; after that, its purpose is finished (see Galatians 3:24–25). I encourage you to put your faith in Christ and Christ alone. The law will never save you, only condemn you. Look to Christ alone.

A young man was deeply involved in the drug culture, and he had tried everything there was to try from marijuana to mushrooms, from hash to heroin. He was hopelessly addicted and he knew it. He tried many times to stop, went through drug recovery programs, read dozens of self–help books, and tried hypnosis. In his desperation for relief from his torment, he had even attempted suicide. He was no more successful there than in his feeble attempts to stop using drugs.

One evening, at dusk, the young man, weary of his lifestyle and unsuccessful efforts to change it, drove his car to the edge of town and up a hillside to an overlook which offered a panoramic view of the valley below. On the top of the hill stood a larger–than–life statue of Christ, arms outstretched in a gesture of loving acceptance. The young man carefully assembled all of his drug paraphernalia then stepped out of his car. He carried his hypodermic needles and an assortment of illegal drugs in a paper bag. He slowly yet deliberately walked to the foot of the statue where he knelt down and emptied the bag. Spreading out all his paraphernalia and hundreds of dollars of drugs in front of him, in plain view, he earnestly began to pray for deliverance. He prayed like he had as a child, a simple prayer, a prayer of faith, as he poured out his heart to the One represented by the cement statue now towering over him. He begged to be set free from the bondage which had enslaved him for many, many years.

The kneeling figure was hardly noticeable as dusk turned into evening. He was so deeply in prayer that he did not hear the approaching police car until it pulled into the nearby parking lot. A powerful searchlight swept the area where he knelt, distracting him from his private thoughts. He glanced behind himself and saw two uniformed officers step from their patrol car. Their flashlights illuminated him as they approached. His heart began to pound and his breath quickened. He quickly thought of trying to hide his stash, but it was pointless. He had been seen, and the evidence of his transgressions was spread right there in front of him on the ground. He imagined the tight handcuffs, the humiliating body search, and the jarring sound of the jail door slamming shut. The awful *clank*. He pictured himself in prison for the rest of his life, a hopeless repeat offender. A cold sweat broke out on his forehead and he felt sick to his stomach. He thought of running, but where would he hide?

With no way of escape, the young man resigned himself to inevitable capture, prosecution, conviction, and incarceration. With nowhere else to turn, he silently bowed his head and prayed even more fervently to be cured of his drug addiction. As he prayed, he heard two sets of footsteps draw nearer until they stopped right behind him. He felt their presence, though neither one spoke a word. Their mere presence made him sense more than ever his sinfulness and depravity. He continued to pray as he knelt before the strong symbol of the Redeemer. He prayed with all his might. He asked for forgiveness for a life wasted. He pleaded for power to live a clean life, and he sought assurance for his eternal destiny.

He was praying so intently he did not notice the two policemen slowly turn and walk quietly back to their cruiser. The sound of the car doors slamming shut jolted him from his prayer. He listened carefully as the patrol car turned and drove slowly out of the parking lot and down the hillside. He carefully opened one eye and then the other. The young man rose to his feet and looked around. Then he realized the law was gone. . . and there was only Christ.[24]

REFLECTION

How does comparing the law to bathroom scales help to explain its purpose?

How does it change my view of the law to think of it as given not to make me better but to show me my problem and need?

DAY 24

A NEW STATUS
IN CHRIST

Imagine you live in a time long ago and far away, a time when horse-drawn carriages travel cobblestone streets, a time when winters are cold (except by the fire), and nights are dark (expect by the lantern). Now imagine you are a small child of poverty and great misfortune—you do not know who your father is, and you have heard your mother is a prostitute who sold you into slavery for a few dollars. You have no love in your life, no family, no friends, no free time, no hope—only work. Your harsh taskmaster and owner put you to work in a factory, and since you are too small to do anything else, your job is to carry buckets of coal to the steelworkers, twelve hours every day. There is no social interaction, no rewards or incentives, no appreciation—just hard labor. At night you are all alone. You are always hungry, always fearful, always insecure.

One day your master pulls you away from your task and orders you to quickly deliver a letter for him. You clean your grimy hands as best you can and then run to make the delivery. Fearful of punishment, you run as fast as your ten–year–old legs will carry you, but in your haste to cross a street you trip and fall headlong into a mud puddle. Before you can make it to your feet a stranger is there helping you up and wiping the mud out of your eyes with his sleeve. Your first impulse is fear, until you look into his kind and gentle eyes. The obviously wealthy gentleman lifts you into his carriage for a conversation. When he learns you have no parents he asks you many questions. He tells you he has no children; therefore he has no heir. He has been looking for a child to be his son, to live in his castle, to eat at his table, and to inherit everything he owns.

The wealthy gentleman arranges for your release, paying the greedy master far more than a fair amount. He takes you to his castle and introduces you to your tutor, a strict disciplinarian who will teach you manners and the rules of the house. You are not yet an heir with full rights of sonship, but you will be on the day set by the gentleman. Before the gentleman leaves for an extended journey abroad he tells the tutor, "Teach him the basics, the ABCs, reading, writing, and arithmetic. Do not give him full run of the house just yet, for he still thinks like a slave. He is not ready to live as a son."

Sometime later the gentleman returns. He announces the set time has come. A special ceremony is arranged, a coming–of–age ceremony for you, the former slave. The wealthy gentleman brings you before the gathered guests and declares publicly you are his son. "Today you are officially adopted," he says, "You are now to call me 'Father,' not 'Sir.'" He gives you a special overcoat that signifies honor. He puts on your hand a signet ring which enables you to sign checks on his bank account. "You are now my son," he says, "all I have I give to you. You have full rights as a son, now you are my heir."

Can you imagine that? After growing up a slave, how much would you appreciate and value your new status? The feel of that imaginary story is the feel of the passage we are looking at in this chapter, describing a new status, not an imaginary one but very real for all who belong to Christ.

Before the coming of this faith, we were held in custody under
the law, locked up until the faith that was to come would be
revealed. So the law was our guardian until Christ came that
we might be justified by faith. Now that this faith has come,
we are no longer under a guardian. (Galatians 3:23–25)

We have seen the law era was temporary. The law was *added* long
after the promise (430 years later) and only *until* Christ would come
(Galatians 3:19). The purpose of the law was to show the holiness of
God, the sinfulness of humans, and the need for a savior. The law locked
up people as prisoners by turning wrongdoing into a legal offense and
declaring all people guilty. The law had an important but temporary
responsibility.

Verse 24 says the law was our *guardian*. The Greek word there
is *paidagogos* from which we get the word "pedagogue." A pedagogue
in Greek culture was a guardian who took care of little children. The
nuances of the Greek word can be seen by comparing different Bible
translations:

- The law was our *custodian* until Christ came (RSV)
- The law was our *disciplinarian* until Christ came (NRSV)
- The law was our *schoolmaster* to bring us unto Christ (KJV)
- The Law has become our *tutor* to lead us to Christ (NASB)
- The law was our *guardian* and *teacher* to lead us until Christ
  came (NLT)

The pedagogue was a slave whom wealthy families hired to watch
over and discipline their children, take them back and forth to school,
make sure they did their homework, and teach them manners. The work
of a pedagogue was temporary—only until the child grew up. So it is
with the law. It has a temporary function to lead us to Christ. *Now that
faith has come, we are no longer under a guardian.*

Does that mean Christians just throw out all guidelines and moral principles and live irresponsible, self–centered lives? Of course not. We choose to live God–honoring, loving lives, but we look to Christ for guidance, not the law. Christ is a much greater revelation of God's perfect will than the written law on stone and parchments. We focus on Christ and his teachings outlined in the New Testament and follow the guidance of the Holy Spirit (Galatians 5:16–18). The law is no longer our primary reference for morality, Jesus is. New Covenant Christians are no longer under law.

Are you old enough to remember typing on a typewriter? (Maybe you were listening to Neil Diamond on your 8–track player while you typed). The Old Covenant law might be compared to a typewriter and the New Covenant to a computer. The computer is everything the typewriter was intended to be, but so much more. When you use a computer, you are still using the old typewriter's technology, but the computer transcends by far what the typewriter ever could accomplish.

When a Christian lives in the Spirit and under Christ, that believer is not living contrary to the law, but transcending it. Comparing the law to the typewriter, author Scot McKnight writes:

> When the computer age arrived, we put away our manual typewriters because they belonged to a former era. Paul's critique of the Judaizers is that they were typing on manual typewriters after new computers were on the desk! He calls them to put the manual typewriters away. But in putting them away, we do not destroy them. We fulfill them by typing on computers.[25]

New Covenant Christians set aside the Old Covenant law, not because it was bad, but because it has been fulfilled and thus outdated. "Now that faith has come, we are no longer under a guardian. So in Christ Jesus you are all children of God through faith" (Galatians 3:25–26).

Notice the word *all*. That is an important word, and it appears again in verses 27 and 28. The gospel is inclusive, it is for all. Not just for one race, one culture, one social status, or one gender—it is for all. All is a big word. But do not make it too big. It includes *any*body, but not *every*body. It includes anybody who accepts Christ Jesus by faith, but not everybody regardless of their relationship to Christ.

God is the creator of all people, but not all people are his *children*. The Bible states some people are enemies of God, some are called children of wrath, or children of the devil. Do not fall prey to the Universalist's notion that all people are God's children in the sense that all will be saved regardless of their relationship to Jesus, and all roads lead to heaven. Only those who are *in Christ* are saved. Our only safety is *in Christ Jesus*. Once you hide your life in him and accept the free gift of salvation by grace, you are a child of God with a new status; you are completely safe. "For all of you who were baptized into Christ have clothed yourselves with Christ" (Galatians 3:27).

At the Roman coming of age ceremony, the child who was becoming an adult put on a new robe called a *toga virilis*. It was a robe which only adults could wear—that seems to be the imagery here. When we are baptized, we are *clothed* with Christ. New clothing is common imagery in Scripture to represent new standing in Christ. When we become a Christian we spiritually exchange our own clothes—our own attempts at righteousness, which the Bible calls "filthy rags" (Isaiah 64:6)—for the robe of Christ's perfect righteousness, and in that sense we are *clothed* with Christ.

Notice the importance of baptism. We are baptized *into* Christ. We enter special relationship with him through baptism. It is not baptism that saves you, but it is an important response to salvation, a public identification with Christ and his body, the church. The next verse is a classic statement regarding our status in Christ: "There is neither Jew nor

Gentile, neither slave nor free, nor is there male and female, for you are all one in Christ Jesus" (Galatians 3:28).

In Christ we have a new status. All the old barriers are knocked down. The law created separation; in fact, one of its purposes was to separate Israel as distinct from the other nations. But now, in Christ, the law has been abolished as a wall of separation. All believers in Christ are one—regardless of culture, social standing, or gender.

In a culture where Jewish men used to offer a daily prayer: "God, I thank you that I am not a Gentile, a slave, or a woman," Paul takes on those three distinctions and annihilates them. He writes *there is neither:*

- *Jew nor Greek.* That was hard for the Jews to accept. And it is hard for some people today to accept other races, yet prejudice should find no place in the heart of Christians.
- *Slave nor free.* Discrimination based on economics and social standing has been a part of every society, but it has no place in the church.
- *Male nor female.* Once again there is no place for gender discrimination or favoritism in the church.

This statement of equality includes more than salvation only. The Greeks were not accepted as Christians and then given a lesser role in the church. The slaves were not accepted as believers but then kept out of leadership in the church. And women were also granted a new status of equality in the church, including leadership roles. Although it took time in some cultures to bear fruit, the principles laid down in this verse eventually destroy systems of inequality whenever applied.

REFLECTION

What type of emotions rise up inside me when I imagine being a slave set free?

What are ways that barriers still exist that need to be broken down by the gospel?

DAY 25

ADOPTED INTO
THE FAMILY

In the last verse of chapter 3, the apostle wraps up all he has been saying throughout the chapter by speaking again of Abraham. "If you belong to Christ, then you are Abraham's seed, and heirs according to the promise" (Galatians 3:29).

The Jews insisted they had special status because they were literal descendants of Abraham. Paul said earlier the promise to Abraham was to his *seed* (singular), which was Christ. He is the one who fulfilled God's promises, so belonging to him is the criteria for being a child of Abraham, a spiritual Israelite. Literal, ethnic bloodlines are irrelevant. Belonging to Christ is the only thing that matters.

Notice the word *heirs*—that is the analogy Paul picks up on in the first seven verses of chapter 4 to describe the believer's new status in Christ. What is Paul saying?

What I am saying is that as long as an heir is underage, he is no different from a slave, although he owns the whole estate.

The heir is subject to guardians and trustees until the time
set by his father. So also, when we were underage, we were
in slavery under the elemental spiritual forces of the world.
(Galatians 4:1–3)

The Jews, the Greeks, and the Romans of that time all had special
coming–of–age ceremonies when a son reached a certain age.
- For Jews it was at age twelve. The next Sabbath he became
  a "Son of the Law" in a special ceremony at the synagogue.
  To this day Bar Mitzvahs continue in the Jewish culture.
- In Greece, a boy became a man at age eighteen. He was
  officially received into the clan and his long hair was cut off
  and offered to the gods as a ceremonial act.
- Under Roman law the sacred festival where the father gave
  the son his *toga virilism*—his adult robe—did not happen
  at a defined age. It happened somewhere between the ages
  of fourteen and seventeen depending on when the father
  determined and set the time. Before then the son had
  little more rights than a slave. He had not received the full
  inheritance of a grownup son.[26]

It seems Paul has in mind the Roman pattern here in these
verses—describing the status of a young son before the *time set by his
father.* Paul applies this metaphor to the world before Christ came and
to every person before he or she accepts Christ: "we were underage,
we were in slavery under the elemental spiritual forces of the world"
(Galatians 4:3).

What are the *elemental spiritual forces* or *basic principles* (as it can
also be translated)? The Greek word *stoicheion* originally meant a line of
things, like a file of soldiers. But it came to mean the ABCs, and then

any elementary knowledge.[27] Paul is saying during the law era, before the Messiah came, humanity was under the law—like children with just the basics, the ABCs. The law did not bring freedom but rather led to slavery:

> But when the set time had fully come, God sent his Son, born of a woman, born under the law, to redeem those under the law, that we might receive adoption to sonship (Galatians 3:4–5).

Each phrase in these verses is loaded and worth considering separately.

WHEN THE SET TIME HAD FULLY COME

How had the time fully come? We don't know for sure, but it is interesting to examine what was happening in the world. The Romans had extended roads all over the empire which made travel easier than ever before. The Greek language had become the language all over the empire which made communication easier than ever before. And a Messianic expectation had risen to a higher fever than ever before among the Jews. Thus, the world was primed and ready for the coming of Jesus and the spread of the gospel. Remember the father set the time for the son to come of age, so it was up to him.

GOD SENT HIS SON

Father and son were chosen roles within the Godhead where there is perfect equality and unity between Father, Son, and Holy Spirit. Jesus was not a son in the sense that he came forth from the Father or did not exist as long as the Father. Rather Jesus assumed a role of submission as a part of the plan of salvation. Some 900 years before Jesus was born God prophesied, "I will be a Father to Him, and He shall be a Son to Me" (Hebrews 1:5; cf. 2 Samuel 7:14).

BORN OF A WOMAN

Jesus never gave up his divinity, but he literally took on humanity. He truly became a man. He did not take our sinfulness, but he took our humanity. It was necessary for him to be one of his own in order to redeem his own. He was born of a woman.

BORN UNDER THE LAW

That is a significant and important phrase to understand. Jesus was born under the written law—the Torah, the law of the Old Covenant, the Jewish law—all of it. He was born at the end of the law era, which came to an end when he called out "it is finished" on the cross.

That's why Jesus followed every detail of the law:
- He was circumcised on the eighth day
- He was consecrated in the temple after forty days according to the law of Moses
- He kept the weekly Sabbath
- He kept the annual festivals—Passover, Feast of Tabernacles, etc.

In fact, Jesus insisted not one jot or tittle—not the smallest letter or least stroke of a pen—could disappear from the Law *until* he had accomplished and fulfilled it (Matthew 5:18). Jesus accomplished all the law required and fulfilled all the law promised. Jesus was *born under the law*. He was subject to it and he obeyed it perfectly before bearing the curse of the law for us. He was born under the law:

TO REDEEM THOSE UNDER THE LAW

Jesus came to this earth on a redemption mission. He paid the price to set the prisoners free. The high price of redemption was his own blood. As a sinless substitute, his sacrificial death on Calvary's cross atoned for the sins of all humanity, opening up the opportunity for a new status for all who accept the gift of grace.

THAT WE MIGHT RECEIVE ADOPTION TO SONSHIP

No longer slaves. No longer young children. No longer learning ABCs. No longer under a guardian, trustee, or tutor. No longer under the supervision of the law. A new era has come, the era of grace, the era of the New Covenant. In Christ we are sons with full rights. Of course, we are sons and daughters, but the word *sonship* is used because it signifies the one who received the inheritance in that culture. In Christ we are guaranteed full inheritance. That means full adoption; full acceptance; full security; full benefits. We have come of age.

> Because you are his sons, God sent the Spirit of his Son into
> our hearts, the Spirit who calls out, "Abba, Father." So you are
> no longer a slave, but God's child; and since you are his child,
> God has made you also an heir (Galatians 4:6–7).

God has given those who are in Christ the gift of his *Spirit*. The Spirit confirms our adoption and gives us the ability to call God "Father." I do not believe people can truly call God their father unless the Spirit of God is in their life calling out through them. People may believe God exists but still not call him father. They may think of him as judge, king, creator, ruler, but not father, unless the Spirit of God is in their life to confirm their adoption into the family.

Abba is Aramaic for father, and it is a term of endearment. Even today, when children in Israel call their father *Abba*, they mean "Daddy" or "Papa." I heard a little boy in Jerusalem calling "Abba, Abba," in a small store to get his dad's attention. It is also a term of respect which defines the patriarch of a family. Jesus constantly referred to God as *Abba* and taught his followers to call God their *Father*. Because of the specialness of the term, Paul carries the Aramaic word over into his Greek manuscripts and incorporates it alongside the Greek word for father.

It is because of the Spirit coming into our lives and confirming our adoption that we can call God our father and know with confidence we are his children and heirs together with Christ. That is something worth celebrating! Do you appreciate your faithful Father? Do you recognize what an incredible privilege it is to be heirs of God's kingdom because of his Son?

Sometimes we are tempted to be discouraged and think we cannot be a child of God's because of our failures and sins. The well-known missionary Watchman Nee tells about a new convert who came in deep distress to see him. "No matter how much I pray, no matter how hard I try, I simply cannot seem to be faithful to my Lord. I think I'm losing my salvation."

Nee replied, "Do you see this dog here? He is my dog. He is house trained; he never makes a mess; he is obedient; he is a pure delight to me. Out in the kitchen I have a son, a baby son. He makes a mess, he throws his food around, he fouls his clothes, he is a total mess. But who is going to inherit my kingdom? Not my dog; my son is my heir. You are Jesus Christ's heir because it is for you that He died."[28]

And so it is with you and me. We are Christ's heirs, not because of our performance, but by means of His grace.

REFLECTION

How might it change my view of God if I used the word "Abba" or "Dad" to talk to him in prayer?

Is there anything stopping me from believing I am truly a much-loved child of God?

DAY 26

NO LONGER SLAVES

There are many types of slavery. Today many people are enslaved by fear, trapped by harmful habits, ensnared by destructive relationships, burdened by financial bondage, or imprisoned by a dead–end job. All who have not hid their lives in Christ are slaves to sin. And many people who live outwardly moral lives are really slaves to religion, to ritual, to rules, and to the law.

Religion is about doing and doing and never doing enough. Religion is about man trying to get to God, trying to somehow satisfy the Creator, trying to be good enough. That kind of religion, which is the natural tendency of all religion, does not produce freedom. But true Christianity, unlike any other system ever heard of or thought of, results in liberty for the soul. "By grace alone, through faith alone, in Christ alone" sets you free alone.

Galatians was written to counter the Christ–plus–something "gospel" of the Judaizers who were robbing the new believers of their joy. Paul insisted the law was not another method of salvation, but a

"pedagogue" or tutor to lead us to Christ by showing three things: the
holiness of God, the sinfulness of man, and the need for a savior. The law
could not save. In fact, it locked people up as *prisoners* and *slaves* under
its *curse*. The law could not save, but it could show how much we need
a savior. And Christ can and does save. Once we come to Christ we are
no longer under the law. It has served its purpose.

> Before the coming of this faith, we were held in custody under
> the law, locked up until the faith that was to come would be
> revealed. So the law was our guardian until Christ came that
> we might be justified by faith. Now that this faith has come,
> we are no longer under a guardian. (Galatians 3:23–25)

We are no longer slaves, but in Christ we are sons. In Christ we are
grownup sons who are no longer under a tutor, for we have come of age
and received the inheritance of the kingdom. We have full rights as *heirs*,
and the Spirit of God confirms that in us by enabling us to call God our
"Father."

> Because you are his sons, God sent the Spirit of his Son into
> our hearts, the Spirit who calls out, "Abba, Father." So you are
> no longer a slave, but God's child; and since you are his child,
> God has made you also an heir. (Galatians 4:6–7)

Now, after becoming a child of the king, who would want to go
back to slavery? No one, right? It may not make sense for a son to become
a slave, but it is possible. And in fact, that is the very thing the Galatians
were doing by following the false teachers who insisted on allegiance to
Old Covenant Jewish requirements and obligations. So Paul lovingly and
earnestly appeals to the people he loves. The next words we read from
Galatians are a heartfelt plea to the believers he is writing to. His tone

changes from rebuke to petition. He lovingly pleads. So far in Galatians he has been appealing to the reader's mind. Now he goes for the heart, calling his converts *my dear children.*

> Formerly, when you did not know God, you were slaves to those who by nature are not gods. But now that you know God—or rather are known by God—how is it that you are turning back to those weak and miserable forces? Do you wish to be enslaved by them all over again? You are observing special days and months and seasons and years! I fear for you, that somehow I have wasted my efforts on you.
>
> I plead with you, brothers and sisters, become like me, for I became like you. You did me no wrong. As you know, it was because of an illness that I first preached the gospel to you, and even though my illness was a trial to you, you did not treat me with contempt or scorn. Instead, you welcomed me as if I were an angel of God, as if I were Christ Jesus himself. Where, then, is your blessing of me now? I can testify that, if you could have done so, you would have torn out your eyes and given them to me. Have I now become your enemy by telling you the truth?
>
> Those people are zealous to win you over, but for no good. What they want is to alienate you from us, so that you may have zeal for them. It is fine to be zealous, provided the purpose is good, and to be so always, not just when I am with you. My dear children, for whom I am again in the pains of childbirth until Christ is formed in you, how I wish I could be with you now and change my tone, because I am perplexed about you! (Galatians 4:8–20)

Paul's heart appeal—both to the Galatians and to all of us who have responded to the gospel of God's grace in Christ Jesus—is not to go back into legalistic bondage and slavery. Live as children of the King; live in freedom; live in joy. Become mature. Let Christ form his image in you. That is the basic message of these verses, an appeal all of us need to listen to regularly, for the natural drift of humanity is toward some kind of works orientation where we get credit and recognition. As Christ followers we need to keep reading the New Testament and soaking up the gospel promises. We need to keep reminding ourselves in Christ we are sons, not slaves. We must never forget who we were and who we now are in Christ.

Once we come to Christ we are justified by faith and receive full status as sons of the King. We receive the Holy Spirit as our leader, and we are no longer under the supervision of the law. We have moved beyond the basic principles that produced slavery and now live in the freedom of the Spirit. Paul pleads with the Galatians not to go back to the system of slavery and bondage. As evidence they are heading that way, he writes, "You are observing special days and months and seasons and years" (Galatians 4:10).

Throughout Scripture this sequence refers to the Jewish holy days which were important observations of the Old Covenant. In Leviticus 23 we see this pattern: *days* = weekly sabbaths; *months* = new moons; *seasons* = annual feasts; *years* = sabbatical years. The Judaizers insisted the new Christian converts conform to the Law of Moses, therefore, they especially stressed the outward boundary markers of Judaism, most notably circumcision, food laws, and holy days.

Most believers today are not confused about the religious necessity of circumcision or Jewish kosher food laws. But sometimes there is confusion about the role of the Sabbath in the New Covenant. Historically people have taken basically three different theological views in regards to the Sabbath: Continuance, Transference, and Fulfillment.

- Those who hold the Continuance view are the distinct minority who view the seventh–day Sabbath as a Creation ordinance that continues into the New Covenant and even throughout eternity in the New Earth.

- Those who hold the Transference view believe Christ and the apostles transferred the Sabbath of the fourth commandment to Sunday as a Christian Sabbath in honor of the resurrection. They believe the command for observing Sunday is still based in the Ten Commandments even though the actual day has changed in the New Covenant.

- Those who hold the Fulfillment view believe that Christ fulfilled the Sabbath just as he fulfilled all the other types and shadows of the law that pointed forward to him. Therefore, he is our Sabbath who gives us perfect rest when we receive his gospel of grace and trust in his finished work. Regardless of what day we worship, no day is more holy than another day for New Covenant Christians. Our focus is on Christ, not a day.

I have friends I respect who favor each of these three views, so regardless of which view you hold, we can still be friends even if we end up disagreeing with each other. In the next chapter I will show you why the third view makes best sense to me.

REFLECTION

What examples have I seen of someone returning to slavery?

Which of the three views of the Jewish Sabbath makes best sense to me—Continuance, Transference, or Fulfillment?

DAY 27

THE SABBATH IS FULFILLED IN CHRIST

Of the three views on the Sabbath—Continuance, Transference, and Fulfillment—the view that makes the best sense to me in the light of the New Testament is the third view, the Fulfillment view. I arrive at this view from studying the three major divisions of the New Testament: Gospels, Acts, and Epistles. What do each of these sections have to say about the Sabbath?

GOSPELS

The Gospels tell us it was Jesus' custom to go to the synagogue on the Sabbath. Jesus kept the Sabbath. Sometimes the example of Jesus is suggested as a reason that Christians must still keep the Sabbath today. But remember, Jesus kept all of the law because he lived under the law. Christians are no longer under the law, as Paul notes when he writes, "But when the time had fully come, God sent his Son, born of a woman, born under law, to redeem those under law, that we might receive adoption to sonship" (Galatians 4:4–5).

Jesus was *born under the law* which means he was subject to all its demands. He was circumcised on the eighth day after his birth, he kept the Passover, the Feast of Tabernacles and all the Jewish feasts and regulations. Jesus said in Matthew 5:17–18 that not one jot or tittle would pass away *until* all is fulfilled. The entire package was in force until Jesus fulfilled it all. On the cross Jesus was aware before he said "It is finished" he had fulfilled everything (John 19:28–30).

ACTS

The book of Acts tells the story of the birth and early development of the church. The Sabbath is mentioned nine times in the book of Acts. Every time, it is mentioned either in the context of the Jewish Sabbath observance or Christians trying to reach Jews gathered on the Sabbath. With the initial evangelistic thrust of the church, the Jews were the target.

The Gospels describe the behavior of Jesus and the disciples consistent with the Old Covenant law that was still in force at that time. Acts describes an evangelism strategy that involved going to the Jews first with the message of Christ. What about the epistles?

EPISTLES

The epistles were written years later, and they contain detailed theological reflection as well as instructions for the church. Do you know how many times the Sabbath is specifically mentioned in all of the epistles? Just once. John doesn't mention it; James doesn't mention it; Jude doesn't mention it; Peter doesn't mention it. There is zero instruction about how to keep the Sabbath, how to relate to Sabbath-keeping in the various cultures around the Roman Empire, how slaves should relate to masters who want them to work on the Sabbath, etc. Since the Sabbath is only mentioned specifically one time in all of the epistles, we should assume the one text is a very important and defining passage. Before we go there let me remind you of the three different perspectives on the Sabbath I mentioned earlier: Continuation, Transference, and Fulfillment. I want you to have those three different ways of understanding the Sabbath in mind so you can ask yourself which view seems to be stated in the only passage that specifically mentions it in the epistles:

> Therefore do not let anyone judge you by what you eat or drink, or with regard to a religious festival, a New Moon celebration or a Sabbath day. These are a shadow of the things that were to come; the reality, however, is found in Christ. (Colossians 2:16–17)

Of the three views, which one does this text seem to support? As the only verse in the epistles, it must be the defining statement regarding the Sabbath for New Covenant Christians. What Paul is saying to the believers in Colossae is "Do not let people judge you if you are no longer observing the Jewish law requirements such as food laws and holy days—seasons, months, or days—those were all shadows that pointed to Christ. Now that the reality and substance has come, you don't need the shadows. You have the real thing." See how the New Living Translation reads:

> So don't let anyone condemn you for what you eat or drink, or for not celebrating certain holy days or new–moon ceremonies or Sabbaths. For these rules were only shadows of the real thing, Christ himself.

You have the real thing, Christians. Do not stay with the shadows. Put your focus on Jesus. He is your Sabbath and your rest. Do you want to experience the fulfillment of the Sabbath in Christ? Then put your trust completely in him, and trust him alone. When you do that, you enter God's rest. Every day you live in the joy and refreshing glory of Christ's finished work, and Jesus is your Sabbath rest. Jesus was criticized by the religious people of his day for not keeping the Sabbath the way they thought he should. In the context of one of those Sabbath controversies Jesus said, "Come to me, all you who are weary and burdened, and I will give you rest. Take my yoke upon you and learn from me, for I am gentle and humble in heart, and you will find rest for your souls. For my yoke is easy and my burden is light" (Matthew 11:28–30).

Jesus is our Sabbath rest; all that the Sabbath anticipated is fulfilled in Jesus who alone can provide rest, not just for the body but for the soul. There is one other place in the epistles where a form of the word Sabbath appears. It is not the word proper, but apparently a made up word to speak of a "Sabbath–like" rest we experience when we stop trusting ourselves and put our faith in Christ alone: "There remains, then, a Sabbath-rest for the people of God; for anyone who enters God's rest also rests from their works, just as God did from his" (Hebrews 4:9–10).

REFLECTION

What does it mean to me to think of Jesus as my Sabbath rest?

What is the difference between physical rest and what Jesus promised—"rest for your souls"?

THE COVENANT
OF FREEDOM

Imagine with me. The year is 1863. A group of slaves on a southern plantation have just received the news for the first time that they are free. It is late in the year and although President Lincoln made the Emancipation Proclamation on New Year's Day, it has taken time for the news to spread—especially in places where the slave owners sought to keep their forced laborers in the dark.

But now a group of thirty-one slaves receive the news that they are free. It is hard to believe. In fact, some cannot believe it. They scoff at the news and ridicule the messenger. But then someone arrives with some newspapers that are read out loud to the group, and gradually it sinks in that they are free, and no longer slaves. In fact, they can leave the plantation and begin a new life if they want. Some are filled with joy and enthusiasm, ready to start packing their few belongings, eager to leave. But some are hesitant, not sure if they want to be free. They are fearful of what lies outside the boundaries they have come to know. There is a certain amount of security they have derived from the established patterns and routines of their life. They are reluctant to admit it, or maybe unable to articulate it, but they are afraid to leave, fearful of freedom.

Many in the group of thirty-one slaves have been together for a long time. Although few are related by blood, they have bonded as a close–knit family. They have lived together, worked together, and shared life's joys and sorrows. They do not want to be split up.

After time for discussion and reflection, a senior leader addresses the group. "We have all accepted the fact that we are free," he says. "Now it is time to do something about it. It is not enough for us to know it; we must act on it. Let us leave this place and go live as free men and women, and let us all do it together. We love each other as family, and we do not want to leave anyone behind. We can live in the same area, earn money as laborers, and then pool our resources and buy some property. We can divide it amongst ourselves and work the land together."

After a lengthy and sometimes heated discussion it becomes apparent the group is not totally united. A small but vocal group want to stay in slavery. They know what they have on the plantation, and they fear things could be worse outside.

Finally, the recognized leader makes a last appeal to the group. "Friends," he pleads, "Let's stay together. Maintaining our unity is a high priority; it's a strong value we share. But," he continues with conviction, "staying together is not our highest priority—freedom is! The majority of us are committed to freedom no matter what the cost. We want it for ourselves and we want to raise our children in liberty. So, each person needs to decide for themselves. We leave tomorrow."

The next day as a caravan prepares to leave the plantation there are mixed emotions. The twenty-four who are leaving are filled with excitement and anticipation, but they are sad inside as well because they hate to leave behind the seven who insist on staying slaves. After tearful goodbyes, they pull away. Freedom calls.

Reading that story, you may be thinking, "Why would anyone want to stay in slavery? How could that be?" Well, it actually did happen in various situations during those early years when freedom from slavery was proclaimed in the 1860s. And you know what? Sometimes it still happens today. It was happening when Paul wrote his letter to the Galatians. That's why he passionately appealed to them to stand firm in their blood–bought liberty in Christ.: "It is for freedom that Christ has set us free. Stand firm, then, and do not let yourselves be burdened again by a yoke of slavery" (Galatians 5:1).

That verse is actually the conclusion to the passage we are looking at in this chapter—one of the most important, instructive, defining theological statements in all of Scripture: Galatians 4:21–31. It is a statement about the two covenants (Old and New) which sheds light on what Paul is saying in the rest of the epistle. In fact, this is one of the key passages that helps define how we should understand all of salvation history and relate the Old and New Testaments of the Bible to each other. The passage begins with this question: "Tell me, you who want to be under the law, are you not aware of what the law says?" (Galatians 4:21)

Notice first off there are some who *want to be under law*. There were then; there are now. Perhaps they find security in having things spelled out in lots of detail rather than depending on the Spirit of God to lead them according to the law of love written in their hearts, or perhaps they subconsciously want to feel like their salvation is at least partially dependent on their own efforts.

The Judaizers were teaching a Christ–plus–something "gospel" which taught Christ plus the law was necessary for salvation. They had influenced some of the new converts in Galatia. Paul is addressing that group here: *you who want to be under the law*.

There are still such people today. I know because I used to be one of them. Paul says, Tell me, you who want to be under law, are you not aware of what the law says? The "law" refers to more than just the

Ten Commandments—it definitely includes the Ten Commandments which were basis of the covenant between God and Israel—but the word "law" means much more than that. The law includes all the writings of Moses—the first five books of the Old Testament (the Pentateuch). The law is especially found in Exodus through Deuteronomy because there is where so many detailed laws of the Sinai covenant are spelled out, but the law includes Genesis as well, even though it contains mostly history, it was also a part of what was communicated by God to Moses at Mount Sinai and later written down. There is evidence of that right here in these verses. Paul says are you not aware of what the law says? Then he refers to a story from the first book of the Bible, Genesis, calling it the law.

For it is written that Abraham had two sons, one by the slave woman and the other by the free woman. His son by the slave woman was born according to the flesh, but his son by the free woman was born as the result of a divine promise. (Galatians 4:22–23)

Paul starts with a brief historical summary in order to set up the theological point he is about to make. Abraham and Sarah were childless. God promised Abraham they would have a son who would be the beginning of a large nation from which the Messiah would eventually come. But because Abraham and Sarah were old, it took a lot of faith to believe such a miracle would happen, so they decided to help God out. They came up with their own plan. Abraham slept with his wife's servant, Hagar, and she had a son named Ishmael. Maybe, they thought, Ishmael could be Abraham's heir.

But God was not pleased with that works–oriented approach. He had promised a miracle by faith, supernaturally. Eventually, Sarah did have the son God had promised and they named him Isaac. That is why Paul says one was born *according to the flesh*—naturally; and one was born *as the result of a divine promise*—supernaturally. With that background in mind, we keep reading: "These things are being taken figuratively: The women represent two covenants" (Galatians 4:24).

Paul includes this literal story from Genesis as an illustration. No doubt he chooses this particular illustration because of what the false teachers were saying. They were insisting being a child of Abraham gave special advantages. They were proud in the security they felt in being literal, physical descendants of Abraham through Isaac. But Paul shows them being a spiritual descendant is most important, and he points out it is possible to be a physical descendant of Sarah, but a spiritual descendant of Hagar. That was probably a new thought for the Judaizers. The question Paul raises is "Who is your spiritual mother?" It is still a valid question for all of us because we are all spiritual children of either Sarah or Hagar. Paul contrasts the two covenants using the metaphor of the slave woman to represent the Old Covenant and the free woman to represent the New Covenant.

> These things are being taken figuratively: The women represent two covenants. One covenant is from Mount Sinai and bears children who are to be slaves: This is Hagar. Now Hagar stands for Mount Sinai in Arabia and corresponds to the present city of Jerusalem, because she is in slavery with her children. But the Jerusalem that is above is free, and she is our mother. (Galatians 4:24–26)

There are two different covenants. Where does the Old Covenant come from? *Mount Sinai.* The Old Covenant from Sinai bears what type of children? *Slaves.* While it came from Mount Sinai, the Old Covenant was represented by what city? *Jerusalem*, the center of Judaism. The New Covenant, on the other hand, is one that produces children who are free. It is represented by the heavenly city, the new Jerusalem.

You cannot interpret the Bible correctly unless you understand the difference between these two covenants, and your understanding of Scripture is greatly influenced by how you relate to the covenants.

For example, some read the New Testament through Old Testament eyeglasses. Some read the Old Testament through New Testament eyeglasses. Some say everything in the Old Testament remains in force unless it is specifically untaught in the New Testament. Some say nothing in the Old Testament remains in force unless it is specifically retaught in the New Testament. The approach you take is greatly influenced by your view of the covenants, and the approach you take will determine the outcome of your beliefs.

Even the two divisions of your Bible—Old Testament and New Testament—have to do with the covenants. "Testament" means "covenant." We could just as easily call the divisions in the Bible the Old Covenant and New Covenant.

In these verses Paul clearly contrasts the two covenants—one that leads to slavery, one that leads to freedom. In the next verse he quotes Isaiah 54:1: "For it is written: 'Be glad, barren woman, you who never bore a child; shout for joy and cry aloud, you who were never in labor; because more are the children of the desolate woman than of her who has a husband'" (Galatians 4:27).

This original prophecy was not talking about Sarah and Hagar, but about the Jews who were likened to a barren woman because of their captivity in Babylon. Isaiah prophesies they will be like a fruitful mother after the captivity and have more children than before the captivity. That promise received literal yet partial fulfillment when the Jews returned to the Promised Land after the Babylonian captivity. But true spiritual fulfillment, Paul says, is the growth of the Christian church since believers in Christ are spiritual descendants of Abraham: "Now you, brothers and sisters, like Isaac, are children of promise. At that time the son born according to the flesh persecuted the son born by the power of the Spirit. It is the same now" (Galatians 4:28–29).

Ishmael was born as the result of human works, naturally. Isaac was born as the result of God's promise, supernaturally. In the New

Covenant we are sons and daughters according to the Spirit, not the flesh, supernaturally, as a result of divine promise and grace.

In the original story it says when Ishmael was a teenager and Isaac just a little boy, Ishmael mocked and ridiculed his little half-brother (Genesis 21:9). We do not know the whole story, what all was happening, but Paul picks up on that little detail and applies it, writing: *It is the same now.*

Paul certainly knew of what he spoke. Everywhere he went he was persecuted by those who loved the law and could not tolerate the gospel. Once religious people stoned him and left him for dead. During the Protestant Reformation the same thing happened as the medieval church persecuted those who stood for the gospel of grace, and to this day there is a tendency for those who choose the Old Covenant to persecute those who choose the New. Expect it. Try not to provoke it or retaliate, but stand firm in your blood–bought freedom in Christ.

REFLECTION

When have I or those I know stayed in slavery to the law?

What does it mean to "read the Old Testament through New Testament glasses"?

DAY 29

GET RID
OF THE OLD

I n Galatians 4, Paul is using two women as illustrations of two covenants—the Old and the New. He probably shocked some of the first century Jewish readers when he basically said it was time to get rid of the Old Covenant.

> But what does Scripture say? "Get rid of the slave woman and her son, for the slave woman's son will never share in the inheritance with the free woman's son." Therefore, brothers and sisters, we are not children of the slave woman, but of the free woman. (Galatians 4:30–31)

When Ishmael mocked Sarah's son, Sarah told Abraham *to get rid of the slave woman,* and he did. He sent her away. Now Paul applies that part of the story in his figurative theological illustration. The slave woman represents the Old Covenant. What is to be our response to it? *Get rid of it*—move on. Do not stay married to it; that would be spiritual adultery. Do not try to live with one foot in the Old and one foot in the New. Move on, and be free.

Make a choice. What do you want? A system of slavery or the glorious freedom of the children of God? Who is your spiritual mother, Hagar or Sarah? Are you a child of the slave woman or the free? In his book *Sabbath in Christ*, Dale Razlaff points out a series of contrasts between the two covenants in several New Testament passages, beginning with Galatians 4:21–31.[29]

OLD COVENANT	NEW COVENANT
Mt. Sinai	Mt. Zion
Slave children	Free children
Earthly Jerusalem	Heavenly Jerusalem
No inheritance	Full inheritance
Law	Promise
Works	Faith
Persecutors	Persecuted
Get rid of	Stand firm

Which one looks superior to you? I want to show you a couple of passages where the two covenants are compared and contrasted, showing the Old is over and the New is far superior.

> In the past God spoke to our ancestors through the prophets at many times and in various ways, but in these last days he has spoken to us by his Son, whom he appointed heir of all things, and through whom also he made the universe. The Son is the radiance of God's glory and the exact representation

of his being, sustaining all things by his powerful word. . . (Hebrews 1:1–3)

Notice the contrasts:

OLD COVENANT	NEW COVENANT
God spoke	God has spoken (with finality)
to the forefathers	to us
in the past	in these last days
through the prophets	by his Son
at many times	the radiance of God's glory
and in various ways	the exact representation of his being

Both covenants are from God, but the New Covenant is far superior because it is the final and full revelation of Jesus, God's son. Our focus is now on Jesus, not the law.

Now if the ministry that brought death, which was engraved in letters on stone, came with glory, so that the Israelites could not look steadily at the face of Moses because of its glory, transitory though it was, will not the ministry of the Spirit be even more glorious? If the ministry that brought condemnation was glorious, how much more glorious is the ministry that brings righteousness! For what was glorious has no glory now in comparison with the surpassing glory. And if what was transitory came with glory, how much greater is the glory of that which lasts!

Therefore, since we have such a hope, we are very bold. We are not like Moses, who would put a veil over his face to prevent the Israelites from seeing the end of what was passing away. But their minds were made dull, for to this day the same veil remains when the Old Covenant is read. It has not been removed, because only in Christ is it taken away. Even to this day when Moses is read, a veil covers their hearts. But whenever anyone turns to the Lord, the veil is taken away. Now the Lord is the Spirit, and where the Spirit of the Lord is, there is freedom. And we all, who with unveiled faces contemplate the Lord's glory, are being transformed into his image with ever–increasing glory, which comes from the Lord, who is the Spirit. (2 Corinthians 3:7–18)

Again, notice the contrasts:

OLD COVENANT	NEW COVENANT
on tablets of stone	on human hearts
of the letter	of the Spirit
the letter kills	the Spirit gives life
ministry that brought death	ministry of the Spirit
came with glory	much greater glory
ministry of condemnation	ministry of righteousness
fading glory	ever–increasing glory
veil remains	in Christ it is taken away
bondage	freedom
unable to change the heart	being transformed

That has to be the clearest set of contrasts in all the Bible regarding the Old and New Covenants. Can there be any doubt which one is superior? One more set of contrasts:

> You have not come to a mountain that can be touched and that is burning with fire; to darkness, gloom and storm; to a trumpet blast or to such a voice speaking words that those who heard it begged that no further word be spoken to them, because they could not bear what was commanded: "If even an animal touches the mountain, it must be stoned to death." The sight was so terrifying that Moses said, "I am trembling with fear."
>
> But you have come to Mount Zion, to the city of the living God, the heavenly Jerusalem. You have come to thousands upon thousands of angels in joyful assembly, to the church of the firstborn, whose names are written in heaven. You have come to God, the Judge of all, to the spirits of the righteous made perfect, to Jesus the mediator of a new covenant, and to the sprinkled blood that speaks a better word than the blood of Abel. (Hebrews 12:18–24)

OLD COVENANT	NEW COVENANT
Mount Sinai	Mount Zion
burning with fire	heavenly Jerusalem
darkness, gloom, and storm	city of the living God
begged no further word spoken	angels in joyful assembly
could not bear what was commanded	names written in heaven

anyone who touches is stoned	God the judge of all men
terrifying sight	righteous men made perfect
Moses. . . trembling with fear	Jesus. . . mediator of a new covenant

Is it hard to observe a radical distinction between the two covenants? Is it difficult to discern which one is superior? Notice carefully the personal name mentioned in each covenant as the representative for that covenant—Moses and Jesus: "The law was given through Moses; grace and truth came through Jesus Christ" (John 1:17).

Who do you want to focus on? That is an easy choice for me. My focus is *Christ*, not Moses; *Calvary*, not Sinai; *grace,* not law; resulting in *freedom*, not bondage. I lovingly appeal to you: Live in the glorious freedom of the New Covenant of grace in Christ Jesus our Savior. Do not live in bondage and slavery, under the shadow of Mount Sinai. Stand in the light and liberty of the cross.

REFLECTION

What do I think Paul meant when he said to "get rid of" the Old Covenant?

How does a focus on Moses or Jesus bear different fruit in my life?

DAY 30

CHRIST HAS
SET US FREE

We come now to the keynote verse of the entire epistle: "It is for freedom that Christ has set us free. Stand firm, then, and do not let yourselves be burdened again by a yoke of slavery" (Galatians 5:1).

That first sentence is only four words in the Greek (in this order): "freedom," "you," "Christ," "set free." There is a plethora of good news in those four words! The verb is in the aorist tense signifying a completed, past action. It is done, completed in Christ. If you are in Christ, then you should live in freedom because he already set you free. This is the theme of Galatians, and it is apparent in each chapter we have studied.

- *Christ gave himself for our sins to rescue us from the present evil age* (Galatians 1:4). His substitutionary sacrifice on Calvary's cross was a rescue mission. At the cross he set us free.

- Because he *loved us* he *gave himself for us* (Galatians 2:20). He provided perfect righteousness that is ours by faith. At the cross he set us free.

171

- *Christ redeemed us from the curse of the law by becoming a curse for us* (Galatians 3:13). The law places us under curse by revealing sin. Jesus took the curse and broke its power, and at the cross he set us free.
- *When we were slaves* Christ came and *redeemed us* and gave us *full rights as sons and daughters, his heirs* (Galatians 4:3ff). At the cross he set us free.

The six chapters of Galatians divide basically into three sections: Historical (chapters 1–2), Paul establishes his authority; Theological (chapters 3–4), Paul explains his message; and Practical (chapters 5–6), Paul applies his message. As the apostle transitions to the application section of his letter, he does so with an assertion and a command: "It is for freedom that Christ has set us free. Stand firm, then, and do not let yourselves be burdened again by a yoke of slavery" (Galatians 5:1).

If you have been set free from slavery, stay free. Paul says, *stand firm.* If you are a new believer, freshly delivered from a life of bondage to sin, do not exchange one form of slavery for another by turning to a works–oriented system of legalism. If you are a longtime believer who has come out of legalism into the glorious freedom of the gospel, do not go back to slavery. Stand firm and stay free. At one time you were bent over with a heavy yoke on your shoulders. It has been removed by Christ who set you free. So, stand up; stand tall; stand firm; stay free.

The new believers in Galatia had originally rejoiced in the good news of the gospel—that the loving Heavenly Father had taken the initiative to reach out and save them by grace through faith in the finished work of Christ. They had experienced the joy of forgiveness of sin, release from guilt, assurance of salvation, and security as adopted children of God. But false teachers came along and confused them with a Christ–plus–something gospel. Paul describes them as "false brothers [who] infiltrated our ranks to spy on the freedom we have in Christ Jesus and to make us slaves" (Galatians 2:4).

These Judaizers taught Christ was not enough, that he was only the beginning point, and that Moses must complete what Christ began. It was necessary to observe all of the Law of Moses in order to be saved—all 613 commands found in the Old Covenant. The false teachers especially emphasized the outwardly observable Jewish boundary markers such as circumcision, food laws, the Sabbath, and other holy days (all of which are discussed in this letter). They insisted that new converts to Christianity must conform to these Old Covenant practices in order to be saved. By doing this they imposed an unnecessary yoke of bondage.

The Apostle Paul showed very clearly in chapters three and four that the Old Covenant law given by Moses was a temporary system that ended when Christ came and established the New Covenant. The law could never save; that was not its purpose. Its purpose was to reveal sin and show the need of a savior. Now that Christ has come, the law represents a former era that has passed away. That does not mean Christians are free to live sinful lifestyles (as the apostle will make very clear beginning with verse 13). But New Covenant Christians live according to the law of love, led by the Spirit, not by Old Covenant stipulations.

The *yoke of slavery* is the system of law which leads to performance–based religion, guilt, and condemnation. A yoke is something used for pulling a load, often hard and heavy because the burden is hard and heavy. Or the yoke may be easy and light if the burden is easy and light.

Two other New Testament texts that mention the word *yoke* contrast the difference between the burden of the Old and New Covenants. The first is in Acts 15 where Peter is speaking at the Jerusalem Council. The Judaizers insisted new converts to Christianity must be circumcised and keep all of the laws of Moses: "Now then, why do you try to test God by putting on the necks of Gentiles a yoke that neither we nor our ancestors have been able to bear? No! We believe it is through the grace of our Lord Jesus that we are saved, just as they are" (Acts 15:10–11).

The Old Covenant law with its countless rules and obligations was a yoke even the most dedicated and determined were still unable to bear. It was truly a yoke of slavery, hard and heavy. Now contrast that to the New Covenant relationship Jesus calls us to: "Take my yoke upon you and learn from me, for I am gentle and humble in heart, and you will find rest for your souls. For my yoke is easy and my burden is light" (Matthew 11:29–30).

You cannot walk through life without any yoke. Like Bob Dylan correctly sang, "You're gonna have to serve somebody." So, which do you choose? A yoke of slavery, hard and heavy, the obsolete Old Covenant? Or a yoke of freedom, easy and light, the New Covenant of grace?

Paul appeals to the Galatians and to us when he writes, "It is for freedom that Christ has set us free. Stand firm, then, and do not let yourselves be burdened again by a yoke of slavery" (Galatians 5:1).

REFLECTION

Which form of bondage do I relate to the most—bondage to sin (the flesh) or bondage to legalism (the law)?

In what ways can I "stand firm" so as not to enter back into bondage?

DAY 31

HOW TO STAND FIRM IN THE GOSPEL

Not only does Paul command us to stand firm in the gospel, he tells us how. In verses 2–12 he gives three ways whereby we can stand firm in the gospel. Christian liberty is of great value, is always under attack, and must be protected. Here is how:

1. Resist works–oriented religion

As an anointed, commissioned, God–ordained apostle, Paul chooses his words to convey authority as he warns against legalism: "Mark my words! I, Paul, tell you that if you let yourselves be circumcised, Christ will be of no value to you at all" (Galatians 5:2).

Paul is speaking here to Galatian adult men who were contemplating taking this Old Covenant sign in the flesh as a religious obligation, to try to attain a better standing with God. This text, of course, has no bearing on any modern–day practices of infant circumcision for reasons of tradition, preference, or perceived health advantages. He is talking about the religious significance of this rite. In those days circumcision was understood to be an entry sign into the Old Covenant Mosaic law system. To the church in Corinth Paul wrote, "This is the rule I lay down in all the churches. Was a man already circumcised when he was called? He should not become uncircumcised. Was a man uncircumcised when he was called? He should not be circumcised" (1 Corinthians 7:17–18).

Why did Paul forbid the Gentiles to become circumcised? He forbade them because of what it had come to mean. It was necessary for the new Christians to move away from the signs of the Old Covenant in order to resist the backward slide into works–oriented religion. There are signs associated with covenants. The entry sign of the Old Covenant was circumcision. The entry sign of the New Covenant is baptism:

> In him you were also circumcised with a circumcision not performed by human hands. Your whole self ruled by the flesh was put off when you were circumcised by Christ, having been buried with him in baptism, in which you were also raised with him through your faith in the working of God, who raised him from the dead (Colossians 2:11–12).

There was no reason for the believers to take the Old Covenant sign of circumcision. In fact, if they did so, thinking they were somehow gaining some merit, it would be evidence of legalism. As a result, Paul had some strong words to say here: "Mark my words! I, Paul, tell you that if you let yourselves be circumcised, Christ will be of no value to you at all" (Galatians 5:2).

He did not say "Don't judge. . . let everyone be fully convinced in his own mind," he said, "If you do this, *Christ will be of no value to you.*" Why does he speak so strongly? Because there are only two ways: the way of works and the way of faith.

Suppose a person who did not know how to swim fell out of a boat and began to drown. Now suppose you jumped in and tried to save the person, but he kept thrashing and kicking, trying to save himself. You would not be able to help him unless he gave up on his own efforts and let you take over. You would be *of no value to* him. Christ's offer of grace through the gospel is of no value to one who insists on finding merit through the law.

Every Christ follower must resist legalism. Its consequences are severe. Look at the four italicized phrases in this passage that indicate the consequences of legalism:

> Mark my words! I, Paul, tell you that if you let yourselves be circumcised, *Christ will be of no value to you at all.* Again I declare to every man who lets himself be circumcised that he is *obligated to obey the whole law.* You who are trying to be justified by law have been *alienated from Christ;* you have *fallen away from grace.* (Galatians 5:2–4)

Is that strong language? Surely that kind of wording got the attention of the Galatians, and it ought to get the attention of anyone trying to save him or herself. Have you been slipping into works–oriented religion, thinking you are somehow contributing to or supplementing Christ's perfect work? Beware. The consequences of legalism are spelled out in strong language in this passage:

- *Christ will be of no value to you*—how can he help you if you are trusting yourself instead of him?
- You will be *obligated to obey the whole law*—it is a package plan; if you take part of it you take it all (that is why "circumcision" is just used as a catchphrase in this passage to stand for all of the law).

- You will be *alienated from Christ*—the system of law is a counter system to the system of grace. That is why insistence on the law system results in:
- *Falling away from grace.* Many people think falling from grace happens when they sin; however, that is falling *into* God's grace. Falling from grace is to seek right standing with God based on our own efforts.

My favorite commentator on Galatians is John Stott. He stated it well here:

You cannot have it both ways. . . You have got to choose between a religion of law and a religion of grace, between Christ and circumcision. You cannot add circumcision (or anything else. . .) to Christ as necessary to salvation, because Christ is sufficient for salvation in Himself. If you add anything to Christ, you lose Christ. Salvation is in Christ alone by grace alone through faith alone.[30]

In order to stand firm in the gospel, resist works–oriented religion and:

2.   Put your faith in Christ alone

For through the Spirit we eagerly await by faith the righteousness for which we hope. For in Christ Jesus neither circumcision nor uncircumcision has any value. The only thing that counts is faith expressing itself through love. (Galatians 5:5–6)

Notice the emphasis in these verses. After warning against legalism and listing its consequences, Paul's next words are about righteousness by faith. *The only thing that counts is faith.* The only thing that matters is faith in Christ and Christ alone.

The text says we do not work for righteousness, we *wait* for it. Paul appears to be talking about final glorification. Theologians like to use big words like justification, sanctification, and glorification. These terms are helpful, though, to bring clarity. When you become a believer, you are covered by Christ's perfect righteousness (justification). As you grow and mature as a follower of Christ, his righteousness is manifested more and more in your life as you gradually become more like him (sanctification). But we still depend entirely every step of the way on Christ's perfect righteousness, not our own. At the final resurrection our corrupt human natures will be replaced with perfect sinless natures (glorification). This is what this text is talking about, final glorification, our certain hope for which we eagerly *wait* (not work).

Paul reiterates this concept when he writes, "For in the gospel a righteousness from God is revealed, a righteousness that is by faith from first to last" (Romans 1:17). "By faith from first to last" means from beginning to end. From justification to glorification. By faith alone, in Christ alone. Therefore, *in Christ Jesus neither circumcision nor uncircumcision has any value.* The law and its signs and observances are irrelevant, of no value. What matters is faith in Christ. That is *the only thing that counts.* And notice what type of faith is defined here—not dead faith, not just intellectual assent, but living faith, faith that responds and *expresses itself through love.*

Do you want to protect your freedom in Christ? Do you want to stand firm in the gospel? Here is how: resist works–oriented religion, put your faith in Christ alone, and:

3. Reject false teaching

Paul liked to use sports analogies. He often compared the Christian life to running a race. The imagery here is of someone cutting in part way through the race and causing a runner to trip and stumble.

You were running a good race. Who cut in on you to keep
you from obeying the truth? That kind of persuasion does
not come from the one who calls you. "A little yeast works
through the whole batch of dough." (Galatians 5:7–9)

Paul may well have known who the false teachers were, but he
asks "who?" as a rhetorical question to cause the readers to think about
and evaluate better who they listen to. We all need that reminder. A
lot of false teaching is always floating around. Watch out for a Christ–
plus–something gospel and stay away from it. Avoid reading books that
contain it or listening to people who teach it, for it does not come from
the Lord (verse 8) and it has a way of spreading insidiously like *yeast
working through a whole batch of dough* (verse 9). That is why we need
to beware and reject false teaching and false teachers who propagate it.

I am confident in the Lord that you will take no other view.
The one who is throwing you into confusion, whoever that
may be, will have to pay the penalty. Brothers and sisters,
if I am still preaching circumcision, why am I still being
persecuted? In that case the offense of the cross has been
abolished. (Galatians 5:10–11)

It is a serious thing to teach false doctrines, especially a Christ–
plus–something gospel. Paul reminds the readers of a coming judgment
where those who insist on confusing people with a false gospel *will have
to pay a penalty.* It appears some of Paul's enemies were accusing him
of hypocrisy, saying he preached circumcision in Jerusalem, but was
just trying to make things easy for the Galatians, and that he was not
preaching the whole gospel. Paul responds to that charge: "If I am still
preaching circumcision, why am I still being persecuted? In that case the
offense of the cross has been abolished" (Galatians 5:12).

Notice that phrase *the offense of the cross*. Paul elaborated on it when he wrote, "We preach Christ crucified: a stumbling block to Jews and foolishness to Gentiles" (1 Corinthians 1:23). The teaching of the cross was *foolishness* to Gentile unbelievers who looked to logic and reason, the wisdom of the world. And it was a *stumbling block* or *offense* to the Jews, not only because it made their treasured system obsolete, but because it made their prideful achievement irrelevant.

There was a time when Paul had preached circumcision and all that went with it. He had followed and compelled others to obey the Jewish law, but now he gloried only in the cross, and for that he was persecuted. He closes out this warning against false teaching and false teachers with the severe statement, "As for those agitators, I wish they would go the whole way and emasculate themselves" (Galatians 5:12).

Do you hear what Paul is saying? Emasculate means to castrate, or worse. He is telling the false teachers who are insisting on circumcision to just *go the whole way* and cut it off. Do you think Paul had strong feelings about false teachers?

If you want to stand firm in the gospel then: resist works–oriented religion, put your faith in Christ alone, and reject false teaching.

REFLECTION

What type of false teaching have I encountered?

Paul's words in Galatians 5:12 are surprising. Why would he deliver such a severe statement?

DAY 32

CHANGE
YOUR FOCUS

D id you ever take your kids to Chuck E. Cheese restaurant? Definitely not what most adults would consider fine dining or a peaceful place. Actually, it is bedlam, with loud games and children running everywhere out of control. If I offered to take you out to lunch today and said we could go anywhere you wanted, my guess is you would not pick Chuck E. Cheese. Have you ever been there when it is packed with kids scampering around from game to game, screaming at the top of their lungs, music blaring over the speakers, and then the band cranks up and a bunch of Disney–style bears on a stage start singing? That is hard to take. When my son was young I remember several times going there and leaving with a splitting headache.

As much as I dislike that place, one game I did enjoy playing was Whac-A-Mole. When the game starts, you pick up a black rubber mallet, and the little plastic moles pop up randomly one at a time out of five holes. You get points by smashing them, but as the game proceeds they pop up faster and faster and it is hard to keep up. As soon as you hit one, another pops up, and then another; the faster the reaction the higher the score.

The Christian life can sometimes feel like that game. Sin keeps popping up in your life. If you focus on the sin and keep trying harder and harder to get rid of it, well, it can feel very much like losing at Whac-A-Mole. If you try to get sin out of your life by focusing on it, it will be a never–ending, discouraging endeavor. We all have a battle and struggle with sin in our lives. That is just the reality of living in a fallen world. So what should we do about it? Give up? Throw our hands up in despair? Or should we keep gritting our teeth and trying harder? Is that what we all need?

I suggest what we really need when we feel discouraged about sin popping up in our life is to change our focus. Instead of focusing on sin, focus on the Savior. When you focus on Jesus and let his Spirit work in your life, he does a work of gradual transformation as he develops your character, so focus on the Savior, not sin.

The central message of Galatians is freedom. In Christ we are no longer slaves, we have been saved by grace alone, through faith alone, by virtue of Christ's perfect work alone, plus nothing, period. Some people hear that and wonder if it means how they live does not matter. "Watch out, Clay," someone will say, "all this talk about 'freedom' is dangerous. People are going to think they are free to just go out and live a lifestyle of willful sinning."

Do not miss this: Paul never starts his letters with a call to holiness, but he always ends there, which is significant and important to notice. It is only after a person understands and accepts what God has already done in Christ that any call to morality is meaningful or doable. The only lasting and enabling motive for obedience is responding to what Jesus has done for you. God does not say, "Try to live a good life, and if you do good enough I might just accept you in the end." No, he says, "I have already accepted you in Christ; I redeemed you before you were even born; I want you to be my child for eternity; if you do not push me away, I will save you and give you full rights to an eternal inheritance as my dearly loved child."

When you understand the gospel and accept it, then out of heartfelt love and appreciation for God's loving initiative in Christ, you *want* to respond in obedience, not in order to be saved, but because you are saved—working from victory, not toward victory.

Be suspect of any teaching that jumps too quickly into talk about how we should live, without first clearly affirming how we are impacted by Christ's perfect atoning death on the cross. Only after 117 verses discussing what Christ has done for us does Paul turn to discussion of how we should respond: "You, my brothers and sisters, were called to be free. But do not use your freedom to indulge the flesh; rather, serve one another humbly in love" (Galatians 5:13).

Once more the apostle states his thesis: *You were called to be free.* Then he says, *but. . .* Why does he include that *but?* I believe there are at least two reasons:

First, Paul always got criticized when he preached the gospel. People accused him of just throwing out the law and telling people they could live any old way they pleased. So Paul includes this *but* statement as a qualifier for those who falsely accused him of teaching some kind of cheap grace (see also Romans 6:1, 15). Paul includes this *but* statement to answer the charges of his opponents.

Second, in every age there are those who become "grace abusers" after they hear the good news of the gospel. Grace abusers are those who flaunt their liberty in Christ and take it as license to live in sin, claiming grace as a covering. By the way, if no one is going to that extreme in a particular congregation, then it is evidence the gospel is not being preached clearly enough. No one ever becomes a grace abuser in a legalistic church; there is no chance. Since it happened to Paul, it will happen in any congregation where the gospel of grace is clearly articulated, but just because some immature Christians will abuse grace is not a reason to quit preaching it, and neither does it excuse those who are grace abusers.

In Galatians 5:1–12, Paul declares that Christian liberty is not legalism. Now in verse 13 and onward he asserts that Christian liberty is not license to indulge the sinful nature and live according to the flesh instead of the Spirit.

There are ditches on either side of the gospel pathway. Satan would love to steal your joy and progress by getting you in either ditch, and he does not care which; either one is effective in compromising the gospel and its impact in your life. The ditches are legalism and license. Either one will take away your freedom.

Standing free in Christ does not mean we are free to live without any restrictions on our life, yet that is the way immature Christians sometimes interpret the New Testament message of liberty. Mature Christ followers will never suggest freedom in Christ is license to live any way you please.

Occasionally an immature Christian adopts a libertine attitude. I run into this sometimes. Excuse the language but it comes across like this: "I am saved by grace; therefore, I will do whatever I damn well please, and to hell with anyone who has a problem with it." A person may cheat on their spouse, treat others abusively, practice dishonesty in business, live in unrepentant, willful sin, and still claim security in the covering of grace. But it does not work that way. Grace is accessed through repentance and humility, not through arrogance and pride.

Keep in mind there are people who think they are saved but really are not because they have not fully surrendered to Christ as Savior and Lord. Something or someone else besides Jesus is on the throne of their hearts; they do not have the indwelling Spirit of God in their lives to lead and guide them.

Please do not misunderstand me. Christians are not perfect: we struggle, stumble, and fail. We are all sinners, but when a person is born again, there is an internal desire to live for God, to put away the works of the sinful nature, and to live in a loving way toward others.

> You, my brothers and sisters, were called to be free. But do not use your freedom to indulge the flesh; rather, serve one another humbly in love. For the entire law is fulfilled in keeping this one command: "Love your neighbor as yourself." If you bite and devour each other, watch out or you will be destroyed by each other. (Galatians 5:13–15)

Notice the emphasis here on loving and serving one another. We will come back to this in Galatians 6 where we are told the way we *fulfill the law of Christ* is by loving each other (6:2). Love is the whole law in the New Covenant—loving God and others.

REFLECTION

Have I been in one or both ditches—legalism and/or license?

Which of those ditches is the biggest threat facing the church today?

DAY 33

A SPIRIT-LED LIFE

After establishing the fact that Christian freedom is not an excuse to indulge the sinful nature, Paul spends the remainder of chapter 5 clarifying the difference between two natures: "So I say, walk by the Spirit, and you will not gratify the desires of the flesh" (Galatians 5:16).

Every believer has two natures. We are all born into this fallen world with a sinful nature, *the flesh*. Flesh does not refer to your skin, but your natural, sinful, selfish, fallen human nature. Theologians use the word "depravity" to describe our natural, sinful nature—*the flesh*. If you are a parent then you know firsthand about human depravity. You do not have to teach kids how to be selfish and disobedient, it just comes naturally. It does not take very long after bringing that sweet little baby home from the hospital to discover they want their own way, right now, all the time. Have you ever seen a kid throwing a tantrum in a store? You do not have to teach them how to do that, instead, you have to teach them not to do it. As they grow up, if they are not taught and disciplined to obey, they will become more and more self-willed and defiant.

We are all born with a sinful nature, all in the same boat. It is inherited. What is more, to one degree or another we have all made choices and developed habits that strengthen our sinful nature. But when we are *born again* we are given a new nature, the Spirit of God coming into our lives creates a new spirit within us, as Paul writes, "Therefore, if anyone is in Christ, the new creation has come" (2 Corinthians 5:17).

But it does not take too long after you are baptized to realize the old nature is still hanging around as well, which means each day we must choose which nature will lead us, which nature we will respond to, making it a moment–by–moment choice. When we are walking in the Spirit, depending on his power and strength, we *will not gratify the desires of the sinful nature.* Believers live with a constant internal conflict, an internal war.

> For the flesh desires what is contrary to the Spirit, and the Spirit what is contrary to the flesh. They are in conflict with each other, so that you are not to do whatever you want. (Galatians 5:17)

If you are a follower of Christ, you know all about this conflict. Nonbelievers do not experience this conflict in the same way. Oh, sure, they feel guilt and wrestle over moral choices which may have painful consequences; the Holy Spirit is an *external* force for those who are unconverted. He works from outside as a restraining power in the world, and a convicting voice entreating people to come to repentance, but the Holy Spirit is not an *internal* leader and guide for nonbelievers. At conversion, the Holy Spirit is given to believers as a gift. He is a divine comforter, teacher, and guide.

Because of the Spirit's presence in our lives we live in constant conflict between the sinful nature (the old man) and the spiritual nature (the new man). "They are in conflict with each other, so that you are not to do whatever you want" (Galatians 5:17). What does that last phrase mean? Who wins? Is the text saying Christians will never do evil? Or is it saying Christians will never be able to do the good they want to do? Neither. The nature that wins is the nature we focus on and feed and allow to grow strong.

I heard a story a long time ago about an old Inuit man who lived in the far northern regions. He came into the village every few months and brought two dogs, a gray one and a black one. They were angry fighting dogs. Sadly, the villagers considered it great entertainment and a gambling opportunity. Over time someone noticed the old man who owned the dogs always picked the right dog and went home with a lot of money, so someone went out to visit him and asked, "How do you always know which one will win?" After much coaxing the old man gave up his secret. "It's very simple," he confessed, "I just feed the one and starve the other, and the one I feed always wins!" That is how it is with spiritual things. The nature you feed is the one that wins, Paul notes. "But if you are led by the Spirit, you are not under the law" (Galatians 5:18).

For New Covenant Christians the law is no longer the reference point for morality—the Spirit is. That does not mean believers live lawless lives. When we love God and love our neighbor as ourselves, we fulfill the essence of the law and do so with the Holy Spirit as our reference point, not a law on tablets of stone, or detailed lists of expanded restrictions and commands on parchment scrolls.

This is a scary thought for some folks. Depending on the Spirit to lead us rather than the law feels like risky business, but that is what the New Testament teaches. In order for the Holy Spirit to lead me through my conscience, three things are necessary:

First, my conscience must be cleansed through repentance, an ongoing process which requires repentance and confession.

> How much more, then, will the blood of Christ, who through
> the eternal Spirit offered himself unblemished to God, cleanse
> our consciences from acts that lead to death, so that we may
> serve the living God! (Hebrews 9:14)

Second, my conscience must be informed by the Word of God.
The New Testament is not a detailed list of do's and don'ts like the Old
Covenant, but nevertheless, there are some short lists of activities God
forbids and plenty of exhortations about how we should live, especially
about how we should relate to each other in love. If you claim to be led
by the Spirit, yet willfully live contrary to the New Testament teachings,
you are fooling yourself. My conscience must be informed by the
Word of God.

Third, my conscience must be developed through listening. Usually
the Holy Spirit does not shout; he whispers. As we mature spiritually,
learning to walk in the Spirit, we can learn to hear his soft voice. A person
may have a strong conscience, a weak conscience, or no conscience at
all. People who do not listen to the Spirit and repeatedly shut off his
convicting voice are described as people "whose consciences have been
seared as with a hot iron" (1 Timothy 4:2). That is a dangerous place to
be. Believers are called instead to "fight the battle well, holding on to
faith and a good conscience" (1 Timothy 1:18–19).

In 1 Corinthians 8 and 10, Paul talks about eating meat offered
to idols. He warns believers to be careful not to offend those whose
consciences are weak. Why? Because the conscience is a vital way in
which the Spirit leads, so we should not encourage people to go against
their conscience (even if my conscience does not forbid me). That is
what that whole discussion about meat offered to idols is about—not
offending another person's conscience.

When there is no clear statement in Scripture defining whether a
given activity is right or wrong, there are two key questions a Spirit–led
believer can ask to test if an activity is approved by God:

1. Does my conscience condemn me?

So whatever you believe about these things keep between yourself and God. Blessed is the one who does not condemn himself by what he approves (Romans 14:22).

If your conscience is being cleansed through repentance, informed by God's Word, and developed through listening to the Spirit, and you are feeling guilty about something, then maybe it is not right for you.

2. Can I thank God for the activity?

For why is my freedom being judged by another's conscience? If I take part in the meal with thankfulness, why am I denounced because of something I thank God for? (1 Corinthians 10:29–30)

I heard about a man who quit smoking after understanding the truth of 1 Corinthians 10:30. He tried to thank God for the cigarette each time he lit it up and he could not do it. I heard about another man who was able to finally quit viewing porn when he tried to thank God for that and obviously could not. If you cannot honestly thank God for an activity, turn away from it.

Here is my point in all this: If your conscience is continually cleansed through repentance and confession, informed by God's Word, and developing through listening, then you can confidently live a Spirit–led life. There is incredible freedom in the Spirit, but it is not a life without boundaries. There is freedom, but there is also restriction the Holy Spirit imposes for our own good.

The works of the sinful nature are obvious, yet lest any of us try to rationalize our sinful behavior the apostle provides sample list in the next section of Galatians 5:

> The acts of the flesh are obvious: sexual immorality, impurity and debauchery; idolatry and witchcraft; hatred, discord, jealousy, fits of rage, selfish ambition, dissensions, factions and envy; drunkenness, orgies, and the like. I warn you, as I did before, that those who live like this will not inherit the kingdom of God. (Galatians 5:19–21)

This is not intended to be an all–inclusive list but rather a sampling of the obvious, which is why Paul ends the list by saying *and the like* and concludes with a warning. Please do not misunderstand this verse: it is not saying if Christians sin in any of these ways they will lose salvation. If that were the case, we would all be doomed, right? Notice it says those who *live like this*. It is talking about an unrepentant lifestyle choice. Do not think you can live a rebellious lifestyle of outright chosen disobedience to God and his Word and claim you are saved.

On the other hand, when you fall into sin (and we all do), repent quickly, confess it, own up to it, and then move on. Focus on the Savior, not the sin. Resist discouragement. Do not give up, just keep pushing on, knowing God's grace covers your falling and failing when you are seeking to walk in the Spirit.

Remember this: The best way to get rid of sin in your life is for God's Spirit to crowd it out, not pushed out by you. Trying to push it out is like playing Whac-A-Mole at Chuck E. Cheese. The only way sin goes away is by something better crowding it out. The more we allow the Holy Spirit to fill our lives, the more he crowds out the works of the flesh. But we will be stuck with our fallen, sinful nature until glorification, when God removes sin forever. We will struggle and sometimes fall; we are always and ever dependent on Christ's grace.

When the Holy Spirit is active in our lives, he crowds out the sin by filling us up with the fruit of righteousness, as Paul writes, "But the fruit of the Spirit is love, joy, peace, forbearance, kindness, goodness, faithfulness, gentleness and self-control. Against such things there is no law" (Galatians 5:22–23).

Again, this list, often referred to as "the fruit of the Spirit," is just a sample list; it is not exhaustive. None of these characteristics are natural to our fallen nature. Whenever they appear they are evidence of God's renewing Spirit in our lives; we are becoming more like Jesus. If you are walking in the Spirit, then next month, and next year, you should be a little more like this if you are allowing the fruit of the Spirit to crowd out the works of the flesh. The more mature Christ followers allow the Spirit of God to work in their lives, the more winsome their characters will be.

> Now the Lord is the Spirit, and where the Spirit of the Lord is, there is freedom. And we, who with unveiled faces all reflect the Lord's glory, are being transformed into his image with ever–increasing glory, which comes from the Lord, who is the Spirit (2 Corinthians 3:17–18).

Freedom in Christ leads not to license but to transformation more and more into *his likeness*. Now, after describing the battle between the flesh and the Spirit and listing examples of the obvious fruit of each, Paul ends this chapter with a twofold application. How should believers live?

First, we must continually choose to crucify the flesh: "Those who belong to Christ Jesus have crucified the flesh with its passions and desires" (Galatians 5:24).

Crucifixion was a horrific unnatural death, a painful, slow, and lingering torture. We must daily crucify our sinful nature and say "no" to it, not allowing it to control us (as Paul says, "I die daily" (1 Corinthians 15:31). That cannot happen in our own strength, though. It can only happen as:

Second, we walk in the Spirit: "Since we live by the Spirit, let us keep in step with the Spirit" (Galatians 5:25).

What does it mean to *live by the Spirit*, and *keep in step with the Spirit*? It means to practice his presence, to learn to live moment by moment with an attitude of dependence on God and communicate with him. At the beginning of every day, it is helpful to set aside time for communion with God, but more than that, walking in the Spirit is learning to lift our thoughts to God in all we do, to pray and listen to him throughout the day—while reading the news, driving the car, at work, in conversations—as we go about our ordinary life we seek to *keep in step with the Spirit*.

REFLECTION

How might these two questions help me define God's will when it is not explicitly spelled out in Scripture: "Does my conscience condemn me?" and "Can I thank God for this activity?"

How can I become more intentional about developing my conscience through listening for the whispers of the Holy Spirit?

DAY 34

FULFILLING THE LAW OF CHRIST

Paul spent much of this letter outlining the good news of the gospel—that Christ has accomplished for us what we never could have done for ourselves. Galatians 2:20 summarizes the gospel in two statements: Jesus *loved me* and *gave himself for me*. He lived a perfect life to take the place of my sinful life, and he died an atoning death for me on Calvary's cross. He redeemed me from the curse of the law by becoming a curse for me. He offers me the benefit of forgiveness and eternal life as a free gift, based on God's grace alone. All I have to do is take hold of the gift, and I am *justified by faith in Jesus Christ*. He did that for me. He did that for you.

When you come to Christ you are set free from the tyranny, oppression, and guilt load of the law, you become sons and daughters of the King with full rights of inheritance. In addition, the Holy Spirit is given to you to bear witness within you, providing you with assurance of salvation, and leading you in a life of freedom and love.

After assuring of us of who we are in Christ, Paul goes on to apply the message, encouraging us to live in grateful response to God's grace. "Be free," he says. "Do not be enslaved by legalism—going back to rules and lists. And do not be deceived with an attitude of license—thinking freedom means careless, sinful living. Instead, live by the Spirit, treating each other with love."

Now Paul gives practical counsel on how believers are to treat each other: "Since we live by the Spirit, let us keep in step with the Spirit. Let us not become conceited, provoking and envying each other" (Galatians 5:25–26).

If we are going to *keep in step with the Spirit* and let him manifest his fruit in our lives, then it will immediately become evident in the way we treat other people. *Let us not become conceited. . .* To be "conceited" means to have the wrong view of oneself. In order to "love your neighbor as yourself," it is important to have the right view of yourself. If we think too highly or too lowly of ourselves it will result in relating in unloving ways to others . . . *provoking and envying each other.* These words describe two possible results of having a wrong view of oneself. If you think too highly of yourself, you are likely to have an attitude of superiority. A person who feels superior will try to prove it—*provoking* others. If you think too lowly of yourself, you are likely to have an attitude of inferiority. A person who feels inferior will resent it—*envying* others.

When Paul says, "Let us not become conceited, provoking and envying each other" (Galatians 5:26), he is saying, "Let us have the proper attitude about ourselves so we can treat each other right." The best way to get a proper view of ourselves is to keep a balance between the way God views us outside Christ and inside Christ. Outside Christ we are nothing but lost sinners who are doomed, damned, and deserving of death. If we ever start thinking too highly of ourselves, we should be reminded of how we stand in God's sight if we stand by ourselves. We are nothing.

On the other hand, we need to hold that in balance with how God views us when we hide our lives in Christ, we are no longer slaves, but sons and daughters, full heirs of the kingdom, the highest status that created beings could ever hope for. Loved, pursued, redeemed, brought into the family, and invited into intimate relationship with the Creator, if we ever start thinking too lowly of ourselves, we need to consider the value God places on us by looking to the cross where our worth is displayed.

Nothing will give a person the proper balance of self-esteem and humility like an understanding and appreciation of the gospel. Legalism, on the other hand, leads to "conceit." Legalists end up feeling and acting one of two ways: superior ("I'm better than all the sinners"); or inferior ("I can never be good enough"). The gospel gives us a proper attitude about ourselves which enables us to love our neighbor as ourselves.

With that thought in mind, exhorting believers to *keep in step* with the Spirit's leading and maintain a proper view of themselves, Paul goes on in chapter 6 with some practical directions for how to show love.

Brothers and sisters, if someone is caught in a sin, you who live by the Spirit should restore that person gently. But watch yourselves, or you also may be tempted. Carry each other's burdens, and in this way you will fulfill the law of Christ. If anyone thinks they are something when they are not, they deceive themselves. Each one should test their own actions. Then they can take pride in themselves alone, without comparing themselves to someone else, for each one should carry their own load. Nevertheless, the one who receives instruction in the word should share all good things with their instructor. (Galatians 6:1–6)

Look again at how we fulfill the law of Christ in the way we treat each other: "Carry each other's burdens, and in this way you will fulfill the law of Christ" (Galatians 6:2).

What does it mean to *carry each other's burdens?* At first glance this appears like a contradiction of verse five—*each one should carry his own load.* Which is it? Actually, there are two different words used: *burden* and *load.* In verse five the word for *load* is one used to describe a pack a man might carry on his shoulders. We all have our own load of individual responsibility we need to carry, and we are shirking our responsibility if we do not carry our own load. Perhaps our load is getting a job and supporting our family; perhaps it is doing our share of the housework or helping raise the children; whatever it is, we all have our own load we need to carry.

I love living near the Colorado Rocky Mountains, and one of the best ways to explore the wilderness is backpacking. As an experienced backpacker, I know that one of the first things you learn is everyone needs to carry their own pack. It is the first basic law of the backcountry (and probably one reason my wife has never gone backpacking with me). You learn a lot about people when you go backpacking with them, such as: some people overpack, and some are experts at packing light. We all have a different load, but we all carry our own load when we go backpacking.

But sometimes in the mountains someone's load gets too heavy for a stretch and they need some help. A person may twist their ankle, or bruise their knee, or break a strap on a pack. Then suddenly your *load* becomes a *burden.* A burden is too heavy to carry alone. Do you see the difference between a *load* and a *burden?* Do you know anyone whose load has become a burden, too heavy to bear alone? If so, see if you can get alongside that person in some tangible way and help them out. Be a burden bearer.

I am reminded of that well–known story of the orphan boy who was carrying his crippled brother on his back. An observer asked the boy, "Aren't you getting tired? Isn't that boy heavy?"

Without a moment's hesitation the response came back, "He ain't heavy, he's my brother."[31]

From time to time we have brothers and sisters who need support. *Carry each other's burdens.* For this to work four things are necessary. We must be willing to:

1. Accept help

Being too independent is a pride issue because we need each other, and we must be willing to accept help.

2. Ask for help

We cannot just expect people to always notice or know what our need is. Do not criticize people or the church for not being there for you if you are too proud to ask for help. You must be willing to ask.

3. Give help

It is easy to get so wrapped up in our own world we are too blind to see the needs of others, or we convince ourselves we are too busy to serve others. We must be willing to give help.

4. Follow through

Really helping someone bear a burden may take some time. Think about the story Jesus told of the Good Samaritan (Luke 10:25–37). A man was lying on the road bleeding, certainly a needy case. One religious man moved to the other side of the road to avoid getting involved. Another came along and went over close to look but then went on his way, about as much good as flipping a quarter in the Salvation Army collection bucket and feeling like a real humanitarian. But then came the Samaritan, who got down, showed compassion, poured ointment on the injured man's wounds, bandaged him up, put him on his own donkey, took him to an inn, and took care of him there. The next day he paid in advance for the recovery bill and extended a line of credit. He followed through.

Now notice that verse two says when we carry each other's burdens we *fulfill the law of Christ*. What is the "law of Christ"? That phrase describes the commandment that Jesus gave as the New Covenant commandment. There were 613 commands in the Old Covenant, but only one in the New Covenant. Jesus said, "A new command I give you: Love one another. As I have loved you, so you must love one another" (John 13:34).

The command to "love one's neighbor" had been around a long time (see Leviticus 19:18), but there is something new in this command: *As I have loved you.* How has Christ loved us? He laid down his life. The Creator stooped low to become a part of his own creation. Not only did he become human, but he became a servant; not only did he become a servant, but laid down his life; not only did he die, but he died as a despised criminal on a cruel cross. Christ's love is unconditional, it is proactive, it is undeserved, it is self-sacrificing, and it is unceasing. He calls us to love as he loved, to serve one another in love, to bear each other's burdens, and thus fulfill his law of love. God has made us "sons and daughters"—therefore we are free. God has made us "brothers and sisters"—therefore we are responsible for each other.

REFLECTION

When have I seen how legalism can lead to feelings of superiority or inferiority?

Who is someone right now struggling with a heavy burden that I might help bear?

DAY 35

LOVING CONFRONTATION

A Christ follower will never respond the way Cain did regarding his brother, Abel: "Am I my brother's keeper?" (Genesis 4:9) Fellow believers, we are family, we are brothers and sisters, and that means we care about and for each other. We do not consider ourselves superior and *provoke* each other; nor do we consider ourselves inferior and *envy* each other; rather we love and serve each other. If one is heavy-laden, we come alongside to bear each other's burden; if one falls into sin, we seek to gently restore. This is what walking in the Spirit and fulfilling the law of Christ looks like: "Brothers and sisters, if someone is caught in a sin, you who live by the Spirit should restore that person gently. But watch yourselves, or you also may be tempted" (Galatians 6:1).

The literal translation is *brothers,* not *brothers and sisters.* The term is used frequently by Paul to address his readers (eleven times in this letter). It is not only a term of endearment, but of theological meaning. If believers are all "sons" in Christ, then that automatically makes us all "brothers." The male imagery is meant to be gender neutral, in keeping with the language of that day. For that reason, the New International Version adds *and sisters,* because that is how the first century readers would have understood it. If we are all sons (and daughters), then we are all brothers (and sisters)—which means we are all equal, all important, all family, all related through blood, and we should all stick together. The phrase "Brothers and sisters, if someone is caught in a sin" (Galatians 6:1) has two possible meanings: a believer catches another believer sinning, or a believer becomes caught by sin or entrapped (NKJV, RSV). The verb's passive voice suggests the second meaning, that a believer has been caught or trapped by sin.

None of us is called to be Junior Holy Spirit, spying on people to see if we can catch them sinning. Yet sometimes believers get tripped up and end up *caught* in sin, and while it is not our duty to be snooping into people's lives trying to find sin, sometimes it is apparent that a person has become ensnared. Obvious, persistent sinful patterns may destroy a person and hurt a church fellowship, and when that happens there needs to be loving confrontation.

Confrontation is not usually a word that comes to mind when we think of ways to show love, but it is clearly commanded several times in Scripture. It is not easy. I dread it whenever I feel led to do it. It is much easier to ignore sin issues and hope or wish or pretend they will go away. But confrontation, done correctly, is the more loving way to relate to a believer who is caught in sin.

Confrontation is risky. Sometimes the results are not good. I have confronted people in the past who are still angry with me. Other times it has worked out completely the opposite, and we became closer to each other as a result. I remember one time I had a talk with an unmarried couple who had started living together. I tried to gently show them how this was not God's best plan for them. At first, they got upset with me, but later, after more reflection and discussion, they decided the right

thing was to live separately until marriage. Later, they broke up, deciding
it was not a good match. One of them met with me later to thank me for
speaking straight to them. In that case, it was not easy to confront, but
it was the right thing, and the loving thing.

If confrontation is done improperly, it can produce great damage.
Let us look at four vital essentials for loving confrontation. Confrontation
must be done:

1.   By Spirit–led persons (*you who are spiritual*).

A confronter must be Spirit led. Someone who is living in sin has
no business telling someone else about their sin. The text says *you who
are spiritual*. Now before you interpret that as just super–holy people
or only the leaders of the church, stop and consider the context. Who
are those *who are spiritual*? They are described in Galatians 5:22–25 not
as perfect people but Spirit–led believers. All of you who are not being
dominated by the sinful nature are instead led by the Spirit. You are
spiritual.

That means this command is for all believers, not just pastors or
leaders—*you*. It is easier to pass the buck to the pastor, or gossip about
someone's problem under the guise of passing on a "prayer request."
This is not the biblical method for resolution Jesus gave us for dealing
with problems with others: "If your brother or sister sins, go and point
out their fault, just between the two of you. If they listen to you, you
have won them over" (Matthew 18:15). Jesus tells us to go one-on-one,
privately. Please do not tell others about it if you have not followed
Matthew 18:15. Go repeatedly if necessary. If resolution and a road to
recovery is found, then you have helped your brother or sister, and no
one else ever needs to know about it.

2.   With gentleness (*gently*)

The word here for *gentle* comes from the same Greek word used
back in 5:23. Gentleness is a fruit of the Spirit, though not a virtue

much extolled in our culture, especially for men. But gentleness is not effeminate, it is Christlike. Study the life Jesus modeled where there is obvious gentleness in the way he treated people—children, irreligious people, prostitutes, tax collectors, disciples, even critical religious leaders.

Take for the example the story of the woman caught in adultery (John 8:1–11). The religious leaders were attempting to trap Jesus by asking if they should stone her according to the Law of Moses. Jesus was gentle with the accusers when he said, "Let any one of you who is without sin be the first to throw a stone at her" (John 8:7). Then, after they looked at whatever he was writing in the sand (maybe their sins), and left one by one, Jesus was gentle with the humiliated woman, saying, "Neither do I condemn you. . . Go now and leave your life of sin" (John 8:11). A person caught in sin needs to hear that first message before they are ready to hear the second part.

3. **With a spirit of humility** (*But watch yourself, or you also may be tempted*)

There is no place for a prideful pharisaical attitude in biblical confrontation. We have all done things we are not proud of because we are all sinners. Let us not cop a "holier–than–thou" attitude.

Watching a prisoner led to execution, sixteenth–century English pastor and reformer John Bradford said, "There but for the grace of God goes John Bradford." That is the proper attitude of humility every believer should have toward anyone who is caught in sin. "So, if you think you are standing firm, be careful that you don't fall" (1 Corinthians 10:12).

4. **With a goal of restoration** (*restore*)

The goal of loving confrontation is not to expose, embarrass, or punish, but rather to *restore*. The Greek word for "restore" is used elsewhere for "setting a broken bone, mending a fishing net, or refitting a ship after a difficult voyage." Do you catch the flavor of this word? It means helping someone find healing, rehabilitation, and recovery, so they can be healthy and useful once again in the kingdom, which is always the goal of biblical confrontation.

If a believer is involved in an open lifestyle of unrepentant sin with potentially serious consequences for the individual or the church, they should be lovingly confronted. The confrontation should be done by a Spirit–led believer, with gentleness, with a spirit of humility and with a goal of restoration. Galatians 6:1 is a loaded verse!

REFLECTION

Have I ever lovingly confronted someone or been confronted? What was the outcome?

When have I seen confrontation go well and be restorative?

DAY 36

YOU REAP
WHAT
YOU SOW

I have a cousin who is a police officer, and once he posted a story on Facebook that caused quite a bit of laughter:

Sometimes, when you need it most, the Police gods just smile down upon those in blue. Yesterday, I was just finishing up notes from a traffic stop when a car drove by me. I know they didn't think I had my window down and from their angle, I'm sure they thought I was still in the middle of my stop, when in fact, the violator had already driven off. The front seat passenger leaned out of his window and yelled something to the effect of "F- you f-ing pigs. F- the police." It was at that time, I noticed he was not properly restrained in a seatbelt as required. At the next intersection, I watched the driver shoot across three lanes of traffic without signaling, almost causing an accident because she was trying to make a U-turn where prohibited. Can't have that, right? After all, traffic safety is a division goal. The heaven's opened and a great light shown down upon me when dispatch advised that my man in the front passenger seat had a warrant. Funny, he had nothing to say the rest of our contact. Have a good thought and a smile on me today brothers and sisters! Stay safe!

The first comment under that post said, "Karma is a beautiful thing," followed by several other karma comments. What is karma? Technically, karma is a belief that whatever you do will come back to you, either in this life or the next. Embraced by followers of Buddhism, Hinduism, and others around the world, it is the idea that the sum of a person's actions in the past will impact their fate in future experiences. In some eastern religions that espouse reincarnation, this is extended to previous or future lives, so technically Bible–based believers do not believe in karma. But karma has informally become known in our culture as destiny or fate, cause and effect, "what goes around comes around," and in that sense of the meaning we do believe in karma, although a better way to define is with the biblical language we find in the next verse in Galatians: "Do not be deceived: God cannot be mocked. A man reaps what he sows" (Galatians 6:7).

A basic law of the universe is "what goes up must come down." In the Bible it is *a man reaps what he sows*. That is an undeniable principle, true in the natural realm, the moral realm, and the eternal realm.

It is true, of course, in the natural realm. If you plant a garden or a lawn or a field, what grows is determined by what is planted. You cannot plant corn seed and expect tomatoes. You do not plant wheat and hope to harvest alfalfa. You reap what you sow.

This principle is also true in the moral realm. The verse begins by saying *Do not be deceived: God cannot be mocked*. Do not think you will somehow end up with a mature Christian character and strong moral fiber in your life if you are not sowing accordingly. You reap what you sow. That is what the next verse says clearly: "Whoever sows to please their flesh, from the flesh will reap destruction; whoever sows to please the Spirit, from the Spirit will reap eternal life" (Galatians 6:8).

This verse is worth pondering if you are a follower of Christ. The quality of how and what you sow will be automatically reflected in the quality of the harvest you reap. It is a simple no-brainer but a reminder we all need, because we all have a natural sinful human nature. When we are born again as Spirit–filled followers of Christ we are given a new nature, a spiritual nature, but we still have the old nature, and the two war against each other. We must be reminded of this principle if we wish to develop Christlike character, which does not happen automatically. In fact, there is a constant bombardment with temptations to sow seed to please the sinful nature and a threefold pull toward the pathway of destruction: the *flesh*, the *world* and the *devil* (see Ephesians 2:1–3).

The *flesh* is our natural, selfish, sinful tendencies which are there from birth, but they are magnified by poor choices, wrong decisions, habits, addictions, etc. The *world* represents those elements outside and around us that are godless yet compelling. It seems like the more technology advances, the more temptation abounds in new attractive forms, readily available through digital platforms. The *devil* is a literal being, commander of an army of fallen angels who are active in the world seeking to oppose God's kingdom purposes and derail his followers if possible.

So, with all the readily available seed for sowing to please the sinful nature, coupled with the pull of the flesh, temptations of the world, and the threat of the devil, it is especially important that followers of God are intentional and committed to habits and patterns of positive seed sowing, sowing to please the Lord. You reap what you sow. Fortunately, good seed is available as well. We can surround ourselves with influences that enable positive sowing:

- Spending *time with God* is vital (prayer, Bible study, worship music, nature, solitude, reading, journaling, studying)
- Spending *time with other believers* is vital (corporate worship, small groups, accountability relationships, prayer times, positive friends)
- Spending *time in service for God* is an investment that results in a harvest of positive character development
- Spending *resources to advance God's kingdom* is a way to lay up treasure in heaven and direct your heart. Your heart follows your treasure.

Consider how you sow. It is an undeniable reality: *You reap what you sow.* That old adage is very true: "Sow a thought, reap an act; sow an act, reap a habit; sow a habit, reap a character; sow a character, reap a destiny." If we just put our lives in neutral morally and are nonchalant about developing a Christian character, we should not fool ourselves into thinking there will be spiritual transformation and maturity in our lives over time. We might fool ourselves, but we will not fool God. The Greek word for *mocked* used in Galatians 6:17 can be translated "fooled" or "outwitted." Do not try and fool or outwit God for it cannot be done. There is a basic law of harvest—*you reap what you sow.*

If the Holy Spirit is whispering to you right now about your life, your priorities, your direction, your values, your habits, your secrets—let him speak. Do not ignore his voice or try to shut him off. Let him do his work of convicting, cleansing, and renewal, and when you hear the convicting voice of the Holy Spirit and choose to obey, there is opportunity for breakthrough and progress in your spiritual journey.

REFLECTION

What is the Holy Spirit whispering to me right now about reaping and sowing?

Is there a new habit I need to develop (or an old one I need to replace)?

DAY 37

WORKING
FROM VICTORY

As we discuss the principle of sowing and reaping, please do not misunderstand. The Scripture is not saying you can earn eternal life if you work hard enough. The New Testament makes it very clear you could never stop doing enough bad things and start doing enough good things to save yourself. Even if you could somehow modify your outward actions enough, you could never change your inner sin problem and fix yourself so as to meet God's expectation for perfect holiness. We are totally dependent on Christ and Christ alone for salvation and eternal life. That is why Paul writes just a few verses later: "May I never boast except in the cross of our Lord Jesus Christ, through which the world has been crucified to me, and I to the world" (Galatians 6:14).

Paul says, in essence: "Yes, I'm going to keep crucifying my sinful nature and endeavoring to sow seed that pleases the Spirit so the fruit of the Spirit will be evident in my life more and more (instead of the natural fruit of the flesh). But I thank God that all along the journey of

Christian character development I am covered by the blood of Jesus. So, I do not boast for one minute in my own accomplishments, I boast in one and only one thing—in the cross of our Lord Jesus Christ."

Christians are saved by the grace of a loving God, through faith in the completed work of his Son Jesus at the cross. In Christ, we are redeemed from the curse of sin. In Christ, we are no longer slaves of sin. Therefore, God calls us to go on and live lives consistent with our new standing as sons and daughters—children of light, not darkness—responding to God's grace with lives that give thanks, working from victory, not toward victory. I first learned that phrase—*working from victory, not toward victory*—from my long–time mentor and friend, Dr. Richard Fredericks. I often repeat it. Someone once heard me say that and wrote me to ask what that phrase meant and for a good Bible verse to support that statement. I responded with "For by one sacrifice he has made perfect forever those who are being made holy" (Hebrews 10:14).

I love this verse. It describes both justification (*made perfect forever* in Christ) and the ongoing process of sanctification (*being made holy*). As we discuss this law of the harvest, I am not saying you must try to reap your own place in heaven by your sowing, instead, I am talking about the realm of sanctification, the Christian life we are called to live after we are saved and justified by faith in Christ.

- Justification = freedom from sin's penalty
- Sanctification = freedom from sin's power
- Glorification = freedom from sin's presence

You reap what you sow in the moral realm when it comes to sanctification, freedom from sin's power and control in our lives. This undeniable law of the harvest is true in the natural realm; it is true in the moral realm; and it is also true in the eternal realm. Even in the eternal realm, you reap what you sow. If you invest for eternity, you will reap rewards that are eternal.

Investing in things that last is investing for eternity. Most things will not last, the temporary, the fleeting, the perishable. Make sure you do not just invest in things that will pass away. You will waste your life if that is all you do. Make eternal investments as well, investing in God's kingdom work and investing in people. Our text concludes the discussion of sowing and reaping with a reminder to invest your life doing good.

> Let us not become weary in doing good, for at the proper time we will reap a harvest if we do not give up. Therefore, as we have opportunity, let us do good to all people, especially to those who belong to the family of believers. (Galatians 6:9–10)

Sometimes when you are investing your life in God's work and in people, you do not see immediate results. In fact, sometimes you do not see any results. It is tempting to get discouraged and quit. At times you may feel you are trying to *do good*, trying to live according to God's values, but everything is going against you. This verse contains a good word of encouragement: *Let us not become weary. . . do not give up.*

Do you need to hear that word of encouragement right now? Are you a single parent trying to provide for and raise children, unemployed and looking for a job, employed but miserable in your job, facing marriage difficulties, infertility, dealing with rebellious children, financial bondage, health problems, unresolved relational conflict, loneliness, anxiety, or depression? *Do not give up!* Read verse nine again: "Let us not become weary in doing good, for at the proper time we will reap a harvest if we do not give up" (Galatians 6:9).

Someone needed to read that one verse today. Make the right choices, do the right thing, even if it is not easy or does not seem to pay off. Do not give up. You will reap a positive harvest that God has for you.

REFLECTION

In what ways am I regularly and intentionally investing for eternity?

When have I faced discouragement and need to hear God's encouragement to "not give up"?

DAY 38

THE ESSENCE OF CHRISTIANITY

As the apostle closes this proclamation of freedom, he will declare what for him is the essence of Christianity. But first he writes, "See what large letters I use as I write to you with my own hand" (Galatians 6:11).

It was a common practice in those days to dictate letters. In the absence of computers, an experienced secretary, known as a scribe, was employed to write neatly and accurately. Paul regularly relied on this service when crafting his letters, speaking the words while another wrote them down. Because God used the apostles to communicate his inspired Word, he directed and prompted the mind of the apostle. The Bible is written in a way that reflects the culture and personalities of the authors, but, through the guiding and guarding of the Holy Spirit, it is direct communication from God—even through the pen of a hired or volunteer scribe.

It was also Paul's custom to pick up the pen at the end of a letter and write a conclusion—to personalize the letter and show its authenticity

THE ESSENCE OF CHRISTIANITY

by his unique signature. Often his hand–written part was short and to the point. For example: "I, Paul, write this greeting in my own hand. Remember my chains. Grace be with you" (Colossians 4:18). But here in Galatians, Paul writes a longer conclusion with his own hand, mentioning *large letters*. Why did he use large letters?

There are three common suggestions. One, because of poor eyesight. After Paul encountered the risen Lord on the road to Damascus, he was blind for three days (Acts 9:1–19). Perhaps this experience left him with poor eyesight. Maybe this was the *thorn in the flesh* he prayed for God to take away (2 Corinthians 12:7). Maybe that is why he wrote with large letters. Maybe that is why he wrote this to the believers in Galatia: "Where, then, is your blessing of me now? I can testify that, if you could have done so, you would have torn out your eyes and given them to me" (Galatians 4:15).

Two, because of poor handwriting. He may not have written much in Greek or did not have the nice style of the trained scribe. Consider what he wrote in conclusion to the Thessalonians: "I, Paul, write this greeting in my own hand, which is the distinguishing mark in all my letters. This is how I write" (2 Thessalonians 3:17).

And three, because of emphasis. In those days they did not have exclamation marks, italics, or bold–faced type. As I read the final words of Galatians, it seems to me Paul is shouting out his message with passion. Even if he had poor eyesight or poor handwriting, I believe he calls attention to the large letters for emphasis. He is saying, "Listen up, don't miss this point, underline this." It is similar to sending a text message in all caps to emphasize your point.

Paul now goes on to argue the essence of Christianity is inward not outward:

> Those who want to impress people by means of the flesh are
> trying to compel you to be circumcised. The only reason they

do this is to avoid being persecuted for the cross of Christ. Not even those who are circumcised keep the law, yet they want you to be circumcised that they may boast about your circumcision in the flesh. (Galatians 6:12–13)

Paul once again addresses his opponents' position. They are focused on an outward religion. He goes on to argue that the essence of Christianity is not outward, but inward: "Neither circumcision nor uncircumcision means anything; what counts is a new creation" (Galatians 6:15). The inward work of God in our life is what counts, not outward observances, rituals, or traditions.

As the entry sign of the Old Covenant, being circumcised for religious reasons in those days meant putting oneself under the Law of Moses, under obligation to the entire detailed law outlined in the first five books of the Old Testament, which we now know as the Old Covenant. As we have seen, circumcision is not the real issue in Galatians. It is a buzzword for the Old Covenant, the law. There was absolutely nothing wrong with it in itself, he writes: "Neither circumcision nor uncircumcision means anything" (Galatians 6:15). But because of what it had come to mean to those people, it was essential they avoid it. Old Covenant devotion produces legalism.

I remember visiting a Jewish synagogue one Friday night in Israel. I had heard how joyous Jewish celebrations are and thought maybe I would witness something like that, but it was quite the opposite. It was a very somber, even depressing service. Of course, it was all in Hebrew, so I could not understand more than a word or two here and there, but what struck me was how sad everyone looked and how somber the Scripture reading sounded, as the reader rocked forward and back. It struck me that without Christ there is no freedom and joy—only hard work.

The primary focus for Christ followers is not the shadows of the Old Testament, but the glorious radiance found in the New Testament.

The essence of Christianity is inward, not outward, and the law is not God's highest revelation, Jesus Christ is. With that in mind let's go back to verses 12 and 13. Let me show you five negative results of legalism:

1.   **Pride** (*good impression,* verse 12)

Jesus had a lot to say to the Pharisees about this. When we think our works will impress God there is a tendency to become proud, "look how good I'm doing. . . thank God I'm not like that person. . . "

2.   **Pressure** (*compel you,* verse 12)

Legalists are bent on making sure everyone else conforms to their list of expectations. They will try to *compel* you to conform. Pressure does not usually happen physically; it happens emotionally, psychologically, and relationally. Legalists pressure by not allowing people to fit in if they do not go by the rules, shunning those who will not conform, or using fear, guilt, and threats to manipulate toward conformity.

3.   **Cowardice** (*avoid being persecuted,* verse 12)

The legalists knew they would be persecuted if they let go of the law and trusted Christ alone, persecuted by the Jews as well as the legalistic Jewish Christians. When a person takes a stand for the cross and declares that Christ's work is sufficient and finished at the cross, legalists will persecute. To this day, whenever someone leaves a legalistic group in order to join a Christ–centered group, there is persecution. People who leave Judaism or Catholicism or any of the various Christian denominations or cults that major in minors and produce legalists may testify of persecution. I know that from personal experience.

Some people try to hide their new allegiance from their family and friends for fear of persecution. That is unhealthy. Be willing to stand up; be willing to take heat for the sake of the cross.

4.   Hypocrisy (*not even those who are circumcised obey the law,* verse 13)

Legalists are often hypocritical because they cannot keep all the laws they aggressively enforce on others. In the days of Jesus, the strictest Jews realized they could not keep all of the law no matter how hard they tried, so they picked certain rules and focused especially on those. Today plenty of legalists do the same, selecting one outward thing and then putting undue emphasis on it, even making it a salvation issue.

5.   Bragging (*boast about your flesh,* verse 13)

If you have ever been a part of legalism, you know there is a tendency to see everyone else as the bad guys, and whenever you can get someone over to your side it is cause for celebration. Legalists are often less concerned with true kingdom growth than converting other believers to their way of thinking. They will even baptize people who are already Christians in order to claim them as converts.

The Judaizers wanted to go back to Jerusalem and give a circumcision report. Paul says they just want to boast about your flesh, they want to claim you as a convert to their way of thinking instead of focusing on taking the gospel to the lost. Paul was fed up with legalism, so he called it like he saw it. Jesus was even more severe with his language: "Woe to you, teachers of the law and Pharisees, you hypocrites! You travel over land and sea to win a single convert, and when he becomes one, you make him twice as much a son of hell as you are" (Matthew 23:15).

The fruit of legalism is not pretty: it is pride, pressure, cowardice, hypocrisy, and bragging. The fruit of the gospel is just the opposite:

- **Humility** rather than pride or bragging (trusting Christ alone)
- **Gentleness** rather than pressure (letting people have time, follow their convictions, be led by the Spirit)

- **Courage** rather than cowardice (boldly standing for the cross of Christ no matter what the cost)
- **Genuineness** rather than hypocrisy (admitting one's shortcomings and depending on God's grace while seeking to live a Spirit–led life)

Unlike the fruit of legalism, the fruit of the gospel is attractive and gives gospel–loving Christian an opportunity to boast, and we should boast, but in one thing alone: "May I never boast except in the cross of our Lord Jesus Christ, through which the world has been crucified to me, and I to the world" (Galatians 6:14).

REFLECTION

What does "the essence of Christianity is internal not external" mean to me?

When have I seen any of these characteristics of legalism: pride, pressure, cowardice, hypocrisy, bragging?

DAY 39

WHAT SETS CHRISTIANITY APART

What do you do when you see someone asking for a handout, begging for money at a stoplight, holding up a little "will work for food" sign? Do you give something? And if you do, do you do it all the time, sometimes, or never? I do not give beggars money very often because many of them look like they are able bodied and could easily be doing something to earn a basic living. Sometimes I feel sorry for them—especially if they are elderly or disabled, and I do give out some cash on those occasions.

I read an article about the homeless problem in Denver. Some of the homeless are mentally ill, but many are not; most are addicts. They are prisoners with little hope of freedom without intervention, living in self–inflicted bondage. My heart breaks for those folks. What struck me as especially sad was that in most of the stories it was apparent the homeless individuals did not have to live that lifestyle. They chose it.

Some have family in the area who want them to come live in their homes. Many have refused help in overcoming their addictions. Some will live with family or friends when the weather is really bad, only to return to the streets. Some have part–time jobs, but they choose to spend their income on their addictions. Most could get out of the weather in the shelters, but they cannot drink or do drugs in the shelter, so they opt to stumble around in a stupor on winter nights before collapsing on a sidewalk steam grate.

It is very sad when a person chooses slavery over freedom, especially when they have been set free and then choose to return to bondage. Yet, strange as it may seem, some Christians allow themselves to slip back into slavery after being set free in Christ. To such people the letter to the Galatians is written. The central message of Galatians is freedom:

- Christ has rescued us and set us free (1:4)
- We have freedom in Christ Jesus (2:4)
- Do not live under a curse (3:10)
- Do not be a prisoner (3:23)
- Do not live as a slave (4:8)
- Be free (4:7)
- Be free (4:31)
- Be free (5:1)
- Be free (5:13)

In Paul's closing words he makes a twofold statement about the essence of Christianity. First it is inward, not outward. Second, it is divine, not human. "May I never boast except in the cross of our Lord Jesus Christ, through which the world has been crucified to me, and I to the world" (Galatians 6:14).

What sets Christianity apart from all other religions is *the cross.* It is not about man trying to get to God, but God coming down to man and redeeming sinners—in the person of Christ at the cross. The essence of Christianity is divine, not human. Galatians 6:14 was Paul's life statement (and I try daily to make it mine): *May I never boast except in the cross of our Lord Jesus Christ.* My salvation is solely dependent on the cross—not a shred of me—so what have I to boast in, except the cross? This is why the number–one value for my personal life and for the congregation called Grace Place is Keeping the Main Thing the Main Thing. That is the cross of Christ.

Paul goes on to say that through the cross we have parted company with the philosophy of the world, "through which the world has been crucified to me, and I to the world" (Galatians 6:14).

We have died to the natural system of humanism and trust only in the divine plan and divine provision. The essence of Christianity is divine, not human; and the essence of Christianity is inward, not outward. That is why the next verse says, "Neither circumcision nor uncircumcision means anything; what counts is the new creation" (Galatians 6:15).

This statement may be understood on two levels: first, the individual level. The particular signs, ceremonies, and practices of the Old Covenant are irrelevant now that Christ has come. What counts is belief in Christ and conversion: "Therefore, if anyone is in Christ, the new creation has come: The old has gone, the new is here" (2 Corinthians 5:17). Being *in Christ* is what is important. When you are *in Christ* you are a *new creation.*

This verse may also be understood on the corporate level. *Neither circumcision nor uncircumcision mean anything.* In other words, it does not make a difference if your background is Jew or Gentile, because in the church God has made a *new creation,* and he makes us all one in Christ. In the church there is no more distinction; all believers make up the new *Israel of God,* which is the church. "Peace and mercy to all who follow this rule—to the Israel of God" (Galatians 6:16).

Do not miss the phrase *the Israel of God.* There are at least three views on what it means:

- Some believe it means the Jewish people as a literal, ethnic nation
- Some believe it refers to Jewish Christians
- Some believe it indicates the church

I agree with that last option. The message of Galatians is that God's church is made up of all true believers, whatever their social or ethnic background. The church is now *the Israel of God*—spiritual Israel—emphasizing the continuity of the covenant with Abraham. There is much confusion about this today in the religious world. Paul made himself clear earlier when he said, "There is neither Jew nor Greek, slave nor free, male nor female, for you are all one in Christ Jesus. If you belong to Christ, then you are Abraham's seed, and heirs according to the promise" (Galatians 3:28–29).

Now, after beginning this epistle with the pronouncement of a curse on those who distort the gospel, Paul ends with a blessing for those who hold to the gospel: "Peace and mercy to all who follow this rule" (Galatians 6:16). The Greek word for "rule" is *kanon*, which means measuring rod or ruler—like a carpenter's or surveyor's line by which a direction is taken. The word comes from *kane*—a straight reed or rod.

Get the picture? By pronouncing a blessing for all who follow this *rule*, he is not talking about some law or rule he just laid down. He is talking about the measuring rod of the gospel—the gospel that sets Christianity apart. Paul says to let the gospel be your measuring ruler by which you define all things. If you will judge all things by the gospel and accept what squares with it and reject what does not, you will be blessed with peace and mercy; so it is for an individual, and so it is for a church. The measuring rule is the gospel, the cross of Christ which produces a new creation. A church will be filled with peace when it walks according to this rule. With that summary, Paul concludes this epistle, a masterpiece of true Christian faith: "From now on, let no one cause me trouble, for I bear on my body the marks of Jesus" (Galatians 6:17).

Paul is not saying "stop picking on me." Rather, he is troubled and grieved when he sees the gospel distorted and his converts going into legalistic bondage.

- That's why he starts off this letter saying *I am astonished that you are so quickly deserting the gospel. . .*
- Later he says, *You foolish Galatians! Who has bewitched you?*
- Then he says, *I plead with you brothers. . . what happened to all your joy. . . how I wish I could be with you and change my tone, because I am perplexed about you!*

Paul loves the gospel, and he loves his people, so he encourages them in this epistle to stand firm in the gospel. Thus he will not be troubled in his spirit, *for I bear on my body the marks of Jesus.* Paul had evidence on his body of what Jesus meant to him. He had proof of his unashamed boldness in proclamation of the cross. He had scars from persecution that showed his commitment to the gospel. Five times he received forty lashes from the Jews; three times he was beaten with rods; and once he was stoned and left for dead (2 Corinthians 11:24ff).

Paul knew what it was to suffer for the gospel, and he had the marks to prove it. Do you have any marks? They may not be physical. They may be relational, emotional, or psychological. I know I have marks. Do not be ashamed to suffer for the gospel and bear marks for Jesus.

Paul ends the way he began, with the emphasis on *grace:* "The grace of our Lord Jesus Christ be with your spirit, brothers and sisters. Amen" (Galatians 6:18).

God's *grace* is ever supreme for the great gospel advocate. It is only in *our Lord Jesus Christ,* and it makes us all sons and daughters of God and therefore *brothers and sisters.* Thank God for the grace of our Lord Jesus Christ, the Main Thing!

REFLECTION

How might I use the gospel as a measuring rod?

Do I bear any "marks" as a result of standing for Jesus?

DAY 40

STAY FREE

Frederick Douglass wrote a narrative of his life as an American slave in 1845. He awakened many to the cause of abolitionism as he told about his experiences growing up in slavery—the beatings, the hunger, the poverty, the dehumanization, the harshness of his owners, the forced separation of families, the hopelessness, the fear, the long hours of hard labor. Eventually, he was able to escape slavery and go on to publish an influential anti–slavery newspaper and influence many, including President Lincoln and other presidents.

He tells of going to the nearby Chesapeake Bay when he was still a slave as a young adult on Sundays, his one day off. There he would watch the ships sailing by on their way to the open ocean. Those beautiful vessels awakened a longing in him, a thirst for freedom. With no audience but God, he poured out his soul, putting his thoughts into words, speaking to the sailing vessels:

> You are loosed from your moorings, and are free; I am fast in my chains, and am a slave! You move merrily before the gentle gale, and I sadly before the bloody whip! You are freedom's

swift–winged angels that fly around the world; I am confined in bands of iron! O that I were free! . . . Oh God, save me! God, deliver me! Let me by free![32]

That desire for freedom is in the heart of every living being. God created us for liberty, and whenever a form of bondage occurs it stifles the soul. Let me remind you of the key verse of Galatians: "It is for freedom that Christ has set us free. Stand firm, then, and do not let yourselves be burdened again by a yoke of slavery" (Galatians 5:1).

In that exhortation, Paul not only proclaims freedom in Christ, but also exhorts believers to stay free, to not go back into bondage. It cost the blood of Jesus for you to be free. Do not take that lightly.

On January 1, 1863, when President Abraham Lincoln signed the Emancipation Proclamation, hundreds of thousands of men had already shed their blood to keep the union together and to defeat slavery in our nation. It was a momentous moment.

As the parchment was unrolled before him, he "took a pen, dipped it in ink, moved his hand to the place for the signature," but then, his hand trembling, he stopped and put the pen down. "I never, in my life, felt more certain that I was doing right, than I do in signing this paper," he said. "If my name ever goes into history it will be for this act, and my whole soul is in it." His arm was "stiff and numb" from shaking hands for three hours, however. "If my hand trembles when I sign the Proclamation," Lincoln said, "all who examine the document hereafter will say, 'He hesitated.'" So the president waited a moment and then took up the pen once more, "slowly and carefully" writing his name.[33]

That moment was sacred because freedom matters. The greatest freedom is one that no one can take from you. Jesus signed an emancipation proclamation on the cross when he gave his life and declared, "It is finished!" If you receive his gracious offer of salvation, you are set free from bondage to sin, the law, and death. You move from slave status to son status. Jesus declares, "Now a slave has no permanent place in the family, but a son belongs to it forever. So if the Son sets you free, you will be free indeed" (John 8:35–36).

Have you accepted the gift? If so, what is your response to this good news? Years ago, I read a story about a slave, Old Joe, who was put on the auction block in the deep south of Mississippi. He was an elderly slave who had suffered abuse for many years. As the bidding began, he began to mutter under his breath. But soon his words became louder and louder. "I won't work. I won't work," he repeated. As the bidders heard his words and saw his defiant resolve, they stopped bidding one by one, until only one man was left who was willing purchase the insolent slave.

The new master loaded Old Joe into his carriage and they drove out of town to the plantation.

Finally he went down a little road that passed a lake. Beside the lake was a beautiful cabin with curtains at the windows and flowers by the cobblestone steps. Joe had never seen anything like it.

"This is where I'm going to live?" Joe asked.

"Yes."

"But I won't work."

"Joe, you don't have to work. I bought you to set you free." (The best part of the story is still to come.)

Joe fell at the feet of his benefactor and said, "Master, I'll serve you forever."[34]

Jesus gave his all to set us free from slavery. He purchased us to free us, and that is reason for worship. Listen to what they sing in heaven where worship happens before the throne of God:

> And they sang a new song, saying: "You are worthy to take the scroll and to open its seals, because you were slain, and with your blood you purchased for God persons from every tribe and language and people and nation" (Revelation 5:9)

I can relate to Old Joe. I am forever grateful Jesus purchased me with his blood and set me free. I could never have earned my freedom. As a result, I desire to worship and serve him forever, and never take freedom in Christ for granted.

Jacobus Jonker, an impoverished prospector who lived in South Africa, walked across his little farm in 1934 looking for any small treasures the heavy rains might have turned up.

> As he slogged through the mire, Jacobus caught a glimpse of an oddly shaped stone, roughly the size of a hen's egg. As he wiped away the mud, it began to look more and more like a diamond in the rough. Three days later, Jacobus Jonker sold his "rock" for a fortune. It was a 726–carat diamond that became known as the "Jonker diamond," one of the most famous gems in history.[35]

How do you think Jonker treated that diamond during those three days before he sold it? Do you think he was casual about it? Of course not. He no doubt guarded it with his life and did everything possible to protect it because of its great value.

If you are a Christ follower, your blood–bought freedom in Christ is precious. It is more valuable than the Jonker Diamond. If you have not taken hold of this precious gift, why not? It is costly, but it is free. It cost Jesus, not you. Christ has already set you free, but it only becomes effective for you personally when you receive his gift of grace by faith. Please take hold of the gift.

For those of you who have accepted the gospel, realize that it is worth protecting. Do not let yourself be enslaved. Christ has set you free. Stand firm. Stay free!

REFLECTION

What is my number-one takeaway from this forty-day journey through Galatians?

I have been "purchased" by his blood and set free. How will I respond to that truth?

ABOUT THE AUTHOR

Clay Peck is the founding pastor of Grace Place, which he started in Berthoud, Colorado in 1996. Clay holds a Doctor of Ministry degree from Denver Seminary and is committed to communicating the unchanging gospel of God's grace in fresh and relevant ways. Grace Place is dedicated to being an externally focused, multiplying church and has planted five churches and sponsored hundreds of children who are victims of extreme poverty.

Clay grew up in Colorado before meeting and marrying his wife, Selene, in college. They have two children—one by birth and one by adoption. Clay enjoys dating his wife, spending time with his children, reading, learning, travel, adventure, motorcycles, overlanding, and enjoying God's creation—especially in the mountains of Colorado. Visit him at www.claypeck.org.

ENDNOTES

1   Martin Luther, *Commentary on St. Paul's Epistle to the Galatians*, Fleming H. Revell Co., 1953, Preface, p. 2.

2   Paul Hiebert, "Conversion, Culture and Cognitive Categories," Gospel in Context 11:4 (October 1978): 24-29.

3   Tim Harmon, "Who's in and Who's Out? Christianity and Bounded Sets vs. Centered Sets," https://transformedblog.westernseminary.edu/2014/01/17/whos-in-and-whos-out-christianity-and-bounded-sets-vs-centered-sets/#_ftnref1.

4   John Stott, *The Message of Galatians*, InterVarsity Press, 1968, p. 11.

5   G. Walter Hansen, *Galatians*, InterVarsity Press, 1994, p. 15.

6   https://www.ou.edu/deptcomm/dodjcc/groups/99A2/theories.htm.

7   Duane Litfin, *Public Speaking*, Baker Books, 1992, p. 57.

8   Ibid., p. 58.

9   Ibid., p. 59.

10 Martin Luther, *A Commentary on Saint Paul's Epistle to the Galatians*, 1838 translation, p. 72.

11 C. Rylie, source unknown, https://bible.org/illustration/jesus-paid-it-all.

12 Stott, p. 37.

13 Luther, p. 67.

14 Stott, p. 42.

15 Luther, p. 78.

16 John Stott, *Only One Way: The Message of Galatians*, InterVarity Press, 1973, p. 65.

17 Douglas Stuart and Gordon D. Fee, *How to Read the Bible for All Its Worth*, Zondervan, 2014.

18 John Stott, *Only One Way: The Message of Galatians*, p. 74.

19 Max Lucado, *A Gentle Thunder: Hearing God Through the Storm*, Thomas Nelson, 2009, p. 122.

20 Stott, p. 63.

21   Ibid.

22   Charles Swindoll, *The Inspirational Writings*, BBS Publishing Corporation, 1994, p. 36.

23   Stott, p. 91.

24   Written by Kent Campbell, based on memory of a sermon illustration, source unknown.

25   Scot McKnight, *The NIV Application Commentary: Galatians*, Zondervan, 1995, p. 184.

26   William Barclay, *The Letter to the Galatians and Ephesians*, Westminster Press, 1976, p. 33-34.

27   Ibid., p. 35.

28   Lou Nicholes, *Hebrews: Patterns for Living*, Xulon Press, 2004, p. 31.

29   Dale Ratzlaff, *Sabbath in Christ*, Life Assurance Ministries Publications, 2003, p. 241.

30   Stott, p. 103.

31   https://www.boystown.org/blog/Pages/story-behind-aint-heavy.aspx.

32   Frederick Douglass, *Narrative of the Life of Frederick Douglass, An American Slave, Written by Himself*, W.W. Norton, 1997, p. 46.

33   Doris Kearns Goodwin, *Team of Rivals: The Political Genius of Abraham Lincoln*, Simon and Schuster, 2005, p. 499.

34   Morris Venden, *To Know God*, Review and Hearld, 1983, p. 29.

35   Charles Swindoll, *Galatians*, Thomas Nelson, 1987, p. 99.

CPSIA information can be obtained
at www.ICGtesting.com
Printed in the USA
LVHW032345030921
696823LV00003B/15